G

THE HUNGER TO COME

THE HUNGER
TO COME

Revised and Enlarged Edition

John Laffin

ABELARD - SCHUMAN
London   New York   Toronto

BY THE SAME AUTHOR

Codes and Ciphers
The Anatomy of Captivity (Political Imprisonment)
New Geography 1966–67
New Geography 1968–69
New Geography 1970–71
British Campaign Medals
Digger (Story of the Australian Soldier)
The Face of War
Jackboot (Story of the German Soldier)
Links of Leadership
Middle East Journey
One Man's War
Return to Glory
Scotland the Brave (Story of the Scottish Soldier)
Swifter than Eagles (biography of Marshal of the
    R.A.F. Sir John Salmond)
Jack Tar (Story of the English Sailor)
Tommy Atkins (Story of the English Soldier)
Surgeons in the Field (History of Military Medicine
    and Surgery)
Women in Battle
Boys in Battle
Anzacs at War

ISBN 71747 2
LCCC No. 66: 15597
© 1966, 1971 by John Laffin
Printed in Great Britain by
The Anchor Press Ltd., Tiptree, Essex

LONDON	NEW YORK	TORONTO
Abelard-Schuman	Abelard-Schuman	Abelard-Schuman
Limited	Limited	Canada Limited
8 King Street	257 Park Avenue South	228 Yorkland Boulevard
W.C.2	N.Y.10010	425

CONTENTS

1 The Edge of Calamity Unlimited   13
2 The Human Problem of Hunger   21
3 The Meaning of Poverty   29
4 Population Control and Migration   44
5 What Is Being Done and What Could Be Done   64
6 Trade and Aid   79
7 The 'Green Revolution'   95
8 Education—The Root of the Problem   102
9 The Misery of India   117
10 Asia's Aggressive Attitude   130
11 Fishing; Fish Farming; Food From the Sea;
   Pollution   153
12 World Water Shortage; Salinity; Irrigation   174
13 Trees and Soil Erosion   191
14 Pests; Animal and Fowl Diseases   198
15 Fertilizers; New Seeds; Mechanization   205
16 New Ways and Means   216
17 The Choice for Mankind   229

FOREWORD TO FIRST EDITION

Since the Freedom from Hunger Campaign was launched over five years ago, a number of books have been published in Western Europe and North America dealing with the greatest challenge of our time—how to adequately feed the growing world population. Most of these books are inspired by the moral imperative of mobilizing world action for the eradication of hunger and malnutrition which afflicts a large segment of mankind.

I specially welcome Mr. Laffin's book, *The Hunger to Come*, because the author not only makes a valuable contribution to the understanding of the complex economic and social factors which lie at the root of this evil but is also moved by the human tragedy that is allowed to go on before our very eyes. Mr. Laffin is not content with giving statistical analysis of the problem of world hunger but presents his facts in human terms. For instance, he says: 'There is no sight quite so horrifying as that of a small child suffering from malnutrition or starvation. Even a battlefield scene with its torn, broken and dismembered bodies is not so disturbing, for one can at least find some consolation in the reflection that these men are dead and now beyond suffering.' Again, 'There are also thoughtless people who say, "The Indians (or the Egyptians or the Mexicans) would be far better off if they worked". In most cases they work as hard as their meagre diet and undeveloped muscles will let them—and that is much harder than any Westerner could achieve on the same diet.'

Mr. Laffin deals effectively with some of the problems of

backward agriculture—the lack of incentives, inadequate investment, credit and marketing facilities, archaic land tenure systems, as well as with the broader international problems of trade and aid. F.A.O. policies and documentation in these fields have been widely used, and I am glad to see that the author is in general agreement with the lines of action F.A.O. advocates. The most important and urgent among these is the need to increase agricultural productivity and food producton in the densely populated low-income countries.

I earnestly hope that Mr. Laffin's book will be widely read since it provides a thorough and comprehensive review of the current situation regarding population and food supply and sounds a timely warning about the tragic consequences that apathy or inaction will bring in its train in the not too distant future.

(Sgd.) B. R. SEN
Director-General
Food and Agriculture Organization
of the United Nations

Rome
22 December 1965

FOREWORD TO SECOND EDITION

The peasant farmers in developing countries are in the front line of the world war against hunger. Their ability to advance, their will to produce food, their thirst for and application of greater knowledge and skills are the keys to success. That is why it is so important for the governments and peoples of the richer nations to redouble their efforts to help the poorer nations to help themselves.

It is because he sees this so clearly that I commend Mr. Laffin's book *The Hunger to Come.* Its great merit is that, while giving us the facts about the problems of hunger and poverty, it helps us to understand what these problems mean to human beings—to the hungry, coffin-carrying children in Récife in Brazil, for example, to the children suffering from protein malnutrition in many parts of the world, to the progressive farmer using his new-found knowledge on his small holding.

Mr. Laffin shares with us in the Freedom From Hunger Campaign a true understanding of the difficulty of trying to get the wealthier half of the world to realize how the other half lives, and to feel and care. For example, he writes: 'Normal hunger, as distinct from crisis hunger, is an insidious problem, for people will not respond to it in the way that they will respond to a cry for help following an earthquake, volcano or flood disaster. A catastrophe of this kind captures the headlines and appeals to public imagination and sympathy. But hunger, being ever present and quite unspectacular, arouses no similiar feelings. Help for a national disaster springs from a white heat of emotion and is quite spontane-

ous; help for hunger needs to be cold-blooded and deliberate.
... In this era of the mass communication media, press, radio
and television, it is unbelievable that the wealthier half of the
world does not know how the other half lives, so the apparent conclusion is that the one does not *care* how the
other lives. Occasionally, there is a splutter of over-righteous
indignation or token, even sincere, gestures of horror, but
they come to little. The clammy veil of complacency
clutches, it seems, the whole of the prosperous world.'

Mr. Laffin's book is a sincere and determined attempt to
make more persons understand the problems of world
poverty and hunger, and care more about the people who are
struggling with them. It is a comprehensive and informative
guide to the tasks that confront the world during this Second
Development Decade.

(Sgd.) SIR GILBERT RENNIE
Chairman
United Kingdom Committee
Freedom from Hunger Campaign

London
24 June 1971

AUTHOR TO READER

Twenty-five of my sixty or so books have concerned war and
military history, in all their aspects from tactics to conflict in
the field. I know all too much about the suffering and death
which accompany war. But in the five years since the first
edition of this book I have become increasingly aware that
no war provides as many casualties or as much misery and
horror as the hunger for bread now oppressing this grossly
over-populated world. There would be no point in continuing the metaphor to talk of the 'battle' against hunger. The
battle is over—and we have lost it. We can only hope now
to win the war—though it can only be a war of attrition.
There is no point, either, in being purely objective about the
situation; by investing it with the emotion or feeling it de-
serves we may induce humanity to recognize its peril. The
peril faces us all.

JOHN LAFFIN

Cusop,
Hereford,
England.

1 THE EDGE OF CALAMITY UNLIMITED

Many people who are specialists in their fields have studied the problem of world food and its twin crisis of over-population. Agronomists, biochemists, civic and religious and political leaders, scientists of various kinds—all have, in recent years, made some trenchant criticisms and given some blunt warnings. I have made a selection of their statements to provide a sober, expert and dynamic introduction to my book. The many opinions expressed here are, collectively, far more potent than any one introduction written by a single well-meaning supporter of what I have to say. From them is derived the inspiration for this book and they form, more or less, a brief précis of its contents.

'The Asian's ration is the same Hitler assigned to the inmates of concentration camps.' *Dr. Claude Buss, The Arc of Crisis*.

'Time is not on the side of those who would allow popu-

lations to take their course. . . . The growing restlessness of
populations in the less developed nations becomes more
understandable. We are still teetering on the edge of calamity
unlimited. . . . No nation . . . can escape the threat posed by
the pressure of skyrocketing populations on already inadequate food supplies, meagre industrial development, ram-
pant illness and overwhelming ignorance.' *Donald K. Faris,*
of the United Nations Technical Assistance Administration.

'Nor will peace come to the earth until mass poverty is
lifted and the millions who scratch the soil for a precarious
living can look up and plough in hope.' *I. W. Moomaw.*

'Hunger is more destructive than armies, not only in
human life but in morale.' *Herbert Hoover.*

'It is obvious that if the expansion of population continues
indefinitely it will end in a fierce struggle over the earth's
diminishing resources. To avoid this disaster the birth rate
must be reduced.' *Lord Boyd-Orr,* former Director-General,
Food and Agriculture Organization.

'It may be that the earth . . . will prove capable of feeding
from 10 to 20 thousand million human beings. But this is
only supposition and humanity can hardly be invited to play
poker with such high stakes. Birth control takes some time to
become socially effective, and there is little time to be lost if
a catastrophe in the indigent and overpopulated countries is
to be avoided.' *Pierre Moussa, Les Nations Proletaires.*

'God went walking together with His three sons—a white
man, a black man and a gorilla. The last two lost their way
and God went on walking with the white man only.' *A fable
from the Cameroons.*

'To the millions who have to go without two meals a day
the only acceptable form in which God dare appear is food.'
Mahatma Gandhi.

'A hungry people will not endure reason; they will not listen to justice; they will not even pray.' *Seneca*, 2000 B.C.

'The only practicable limitations to food production are the amount of capital and labour human society is willing to devote to it.' *Lord Boyd-Orr.*

'The first task is to bring to the attention of the entire world—if this can be done—the sad problem of hunger and undernourishment. . . . We are all collectively responsible for the under-nourished.' *Pope John XXIII,* May 1960.

'The most serious contemporary threat, surpassing the threats of nuclear war and political upheaval, is the increasing disparity between food and population.' *N. W. Pirie,* Head of Biochemistry Department, Rothampsted Experimental Station.

'Whether it is moral or not, whether it is possible or not, birth control is necessary.' *Dr. S. Chandra Sekhar.*

'If you give a man a fish you feed him for a day; if you teach him to fish you feed him for life.' *Chinese proverb.*

'The world food situation is perhaps more serious than ever before.' *Food and Agriculture Organization booklet.*

'There has never been enough food for the health of all people. This is justified neither by ignorance nor by the harshness of nature. Production of food must be greatly expanded; we now have knowledge of the means by which this can be done.' Declaration of the Hot Springs Food and Agriculture Conference, May 1943.

'It will need the combined intelligence and efforts of mankind to increase yields, recover the deserts, extend cultivation into climatically inhospitable regions and to farm the oceans which cover seven-tenths of our globe.' *Ritchie Calder,* Professor of International Relations, Edinburgh University.

15

'We have 40,000 regular givers but there is never enough money to go around, and it is ghastly having to decide on priorities. That's why it is foolish to think that private giving can ever be more than ancillary to the governments and U.N. agencies.' *Janet Lacey*, Inter-Church Aid.

'We want understanding about hunger . . . and we want the money we send abroad to make a permanent difference rather than bring temporary relief.' *Donald Tweddle*, Secretary, Freedom from Hunger Campaign.

'Unless the world's soaring birth rate is drastically checked civilization as we know it is doomed. Governments will collapse, law and order will vanish, mass rioting, plagues and disease will sweep the earth.' *Peter Bishop.*

'The world's scientists and planners are faced with a tragic dilemma. What is the good of doctors in, say, India, reducing infant mortality if it only means that the children are more certain to starve as they grow up?' *Professor Denis Gabor*, Imperial College of Science and Technology, London.

'We can no longer say that families should have as many children as they can afford, that all couples have a right to have as many children as they wish. We cannot now, as a people, continue to extol a way of life which . . . will ultimately turn the earth from a habitable place into a grim overcrowded prison where individuals will survive only by stepping over the bodies of those struck down by hunger and despair. . . . And above all we must realize that the time to limit the size of our families is *now*, that the living must take precedence over the unborn *now*, if future generations are to be born into a livable world.' *Margaret Mead.*

'A check on the population increase will come more slowly in other lands (compared with Japan). But it can be achieved. It *must* be achieved if the human race is not to outstrip its resources and find itself with living standards comparable to those of the Dark Ages.' *Gilbert Cant.*

16

'Before malaria was controlled in one area of Africa only two children out of ten survived to one year. After a campaign to stamp out the disease the number of survivors had risen to eight. The doctor responsible called on the chief to receive his thanks and praise. Could he, the doctor asked, do anything else for the chief? The old man said, "Yes, would you tell me who is going to feed all these children?" ' A story quoted by *Sir William Slater, K.B.E.,* and others. It is not apochryphal.

'Our effort will only be successful if people and governments accept responsibility for alleviating hunger as an ethical duty, and it is here that I look for your help and participation.' *Dr. B. R. Sen,* former Director-General, F.A.O.

'There is a definite connection between the minds of ordinary people and world peace because the head, like the stomach, is most easily infected when it is empty.' *Tun Abdul Razak bin Hussein,* Deputy Prime Minister of Malaya.

'Hunger in India is not just an emptiness in the stomach; it is a perpetual pain in the heart. Consciously or unconsciously, it dominates all thought.' *Rawle Knox, Daily Telegraph* correspondent in India.

'When the forests go, the waters go, the fish and game go, crops go, herds and flocks go, fertility departs. Then the age-old phantoms appear, stealthily one after another—Flood, Drought, Fire, Famine, Pestilence.' *Robert Chambers.*

'The great problem of humanity for many decades to come is to ensure that the increase of population stops before the pressure on resources grows too great for a reasonable standard of living to be achieved for everyone.' *J. P. Cole, Geography of World Affairs.*

'The only way the developing countries can break out of their vicious circles of stagnant poverty, disease and ignorance is to concentrate their investment heavily for 10 to 15 years on intense development of their human resources.' *Malcolm S. Adiseshiah.*

'In 6,200 years the present rate of world population would produce a mass of human flesh whose radius would be expanding as rapidly as the speed of light . . . By 2050 the United States will have a billion people and in 800 years there will be one person for every square foot in the U.S. if the present birth rate continues.' Expert witness to a Congressional Committee, 1965.

'Better to walk than to run;
Better to sit than to walk;
Better to sleep than to sit;
Better to die than to wake.'
Eastern saying.

'One can only imagine people either starving in thousands or being forced to fight more and more vehemently to kill each other for food.' *Professor Hans Freudenberg,* medical statistician, Free University of Berlin.

'In a finite world some means of controlling population growth are inescapable.' From a study by Stanford Research Institute.

'. . . the most desolate picture is presented by families who have simply nothing. . . . Not only do whole generations lose physical hardness but, worse still, they fall into crime and wretched moral depravity.' *Pope Pius XII.*

'The most urgent material need of the world today is food. . . . Unless people are fed, the best treaties and agreements can come to nothing. Hungry people cannot be satisfied by anything but food.' *Lord Boyd-Orr.*

'It is past time that the national budget-planners of the industrially advanced nations, and the politicians upon whom rests the responsibility for approving budgets in the democratic societies, recognize that the best and least expensive long-run defence of their national interests lies in the creation of a world in which poverty, deprivation, illiteracy and disease are not constant provocations to violent and destructive upheaval.' *Paul Hoffman.*

'To hear that one in every six people suffers from trachoma, every one of them in dread of losing his sight, and millions in fact, going blind, is to feel overwhelmed by a catastrophe which it is easiest to call an act of God and put outside the radius of one's consciousness. We must not allow the tyranny of size and numbers to blot out our compassion and our will.' *Stephen Hearst.*

'The combined intelligence of modern man can meet the challenge today. Only . . . we have to do it in less than 20 years.' *Ritchie Calder* in 1964.

'Millions upon millions of workless are being swollen by successively larger waves of new generations unable to find work. There is a real threat that whole societies will sink into hopeless stagnation and then most likely explode into violence.' *Dr. Addeke Boerma,* Director-General of F.A.O.

'To couple the concept of freedom to breed, with the belief that everyone born has an equal right to the commons, is to lock the world into a tragic course of action.' *Garrett Hardin,* biologist.

'For the great majority of peasants the benefits of the modern age can be summed up by saying that it has become harder to die. As a result, more peasants are probably kept alive to suffer misery than ever before in history. With appetites whetted by the hope of a better life their present suffering seems all the harder to bear.' *Manfred Halpern.*

'On . . . complicated operations rests the hope of world peace and stability. Yet all too often we proceed by a series of jerky unco-ordinated steps dictated by political expediency. It is easier to stop an insistent clamour for immediate progress by a facile promise than to take the necessary steps towards a real advance, slow and painful as they will be. Yet it is this hard way we must tread.' *Sir William Slater,* formerly Chairman, U.K. Freedom From Hunger Projects Group.

'There are too many people on earth, the United States not excepted. . . . More critical is that numbers of people are increasing faster than we can provide the human services which people need to remain human. We must restrict the increase of population worldwide and we must provide a better way of living for the present and future populations.' *Athelstan Spilhaus,* former Director of Research, New York University.

'The battle to feed all of humanity is over. In the 1970's the world will undergo famines—hundreds of millions of people are going to starve to death in spite of any crash programme embarked upon now. At this late date nothing can prevent a substantial increase in the world death rate, although many lives could be saved through dramatic programmes to "stretch" the carrying capacity of the earth by increasing food production . . . Population control is the only answer.' *Dr. Paul H. Ehrlich* in *The Population Bomb.*

2   THE HUMAN PROBLEM OF HUNGER

Humanity is trapped in the greatest paradox of history. On the one hand people are the only major commodity which can be produced in vast quantities by unskilled labourers who enjoy their work. On the other, these procreative labourers, at least while they are at work, give no thought to the increasingly vast amounts of food needed to feed the exploding population being expelled from the womb with the casual indifference of peas shelled from the pod, at the rate of over one million a week.

They have to be fed from food resources only slightly greater than those available the previous week. In fact, in November 1970 the Food and Agricultural Organization of the United Nations reported that during 1969 food production in developing regions grew at 2 per cent, a slower increase than in 1967 and 1968. In 1969, for the first time in 12 years, there was no increase in the combined production of the world's farms, fisheries and forests. But world hunger is not a mere statistical problem: it is a human problem, a recurring crisis of life and death for millions of real people. Every hour of the day 450 people die of hunger or of its associated ailments and diseases. Somewhere, somebody is dying as you read this page. Equally importantly, somebody else is being born to die—prematurely. So never mind about the statistics. Try putting a face and a name to every soul represented in a number. Then perhaps you will *feel* the problem.

The human problem of hunger can be seen every afternoon in Recife, in north-east Brazil, as groups of children carry coffins through the streets of the peasant quarter towards the cemetery of Santo Amaro. They have no adult company, no parents, no priest and now and then they put down the coffin so that they may rest, and also to show the occupant of the coffin to passers-by. They are very proud of the artistic way they have decorated the corpse with flowers.

The dead person is a child, the former playmate of the young pall-bearers. Each afternoon perhaps 10 children are carried this way to Santo Amaro; the figure rises in the hottest times of the year. At the cemetery rows of open graves are waiting and the children give to a tired official the name and age of the dead child and then while the formalities are being completed they move off to stare at a corpse brought by another group of children.

Finally, when the grave-diggers have lowered the coffin into the ground the children throw in some earth. The burial is completed by the men and the children then adorn the grave with flowers and light some candles over it. All this is done without tears, without any apparent sorrow. Sometimes the children appear almost to relish their task. These children are not callous; they are simply accustomed to such burials and each is aware that he or she may go the same way this week or next month; when you don't get enough to eat you can very easily die of hunger. This part of Brazil, dry and poverty stricken, has 22 million people, nearly all hungry. A person who lives to 40 has had a long life.

North-east Brazil is not the only place where such things happen. In many parts of the world men, women and children are dying of hunger every minute of the day—and babies are being born to die of hunger with even greater frequency. This is the great problem of the mid-20th century—too many people, too little food and an even more acute lack of appreciation of the problem. The threat of nuclear warfare, cancer, the toll of the roads, teenage immorality, sexual promiscuity, financial greed—all have been labelled the scourge of the century. But all pale almost into insignificance when measured against universal hunger and the backgrounds against which this horror has its being. A few, a very few dedicated or farsighted people are doing something about it, but their efforts, though vigorous, are akin to the exertions of a man with a shovel trying to cover up the Great Pyramid with sand.

The quotations and extracts at the beginning of this book are stark and ominous and they underline the seriousness of the situation. It is not too much to say that humanity itself is at stake, if not in this generation then in the next or the one after. Paradoxically, the only people capable of forming an objective view of the position are not those who are starving already but those who have all they need. If a man is hungry, if he sees his children dying before his eyes, he is not concerned with the world situation or with the next generation. He is interested only in the here and now—desperately interested. Survival for himself and his family is all that matters. For this basic reason the world and the future must depend on the nourished man and the nourished country. At the moment dependence on them, for the most part, seems to be a vain hope. Every well-fed person should see hunger in action; then complacency might collapse.

I have seen it. In Cairo one chilly night a black-dressed woman lay down on a pavement against a wall, with a baby in her arms, and very quietly died. Starvation. I saw her lie down and I saw her die and I saw somebody take the baby away from her lifeless arms. In Calcutta I saw a little 'sad baby'—a three-year-old girl suffering from 'the illness with many names'. In Africa it is called 'the sickness of which the first baby dies when the next baby is born'. In India it is sometimes called nutritional oedema syndrome, but a more easily understandable label is protein malnutrition. This deficiency produces a desperate illness, clearly identifiable by the sad, puffy face of the sufferer, generally a child. Ten days feeding with protein-rich foods or with skim milk could have restored the child almost back to health. I expect she died. In Port Swettenham, Malaya, I saw a Chinese lying on the jetty, one arm curled around his head. He was mostly skin and bone and he looked very feeble. Noticing that he was lying in glaring sunshine I said to my companion, a local resident. 'He really ought to sleep in the shade.'

'He's not sleeping,' the man said. 'He's dead. Looks as if he hasn't had a square meal in a century.'

He was an elderly Chinese, probably not worth saving. People sit down and die of hunger in many places, or they die from dieases induced by hunger. Some die on what passes for a bed, or in their fields, which are as starved for nourishment as their owners. A few die in hospital, but a man needs to be specially privileged to do this for a hospital may be hundreds of miles away. Most people who die of hunger or its associated diseases never see a doctor, for what can one doctor do when he has 100,000 patients and a vast area to cover? People develop a fatalism about dying in India and Pakistan, China and South-East Asia, Egypt and the Sudan, in Latin America and Central America. When a man reaches the age of 32 in India, for instance, he knows he has lived his expected span. After that how long he continues is merely a matter of luck.

The world hunger problem is both acute and chronic—and it is getting worse. But trying to explain it to some people is very difficult. I was with a middle-aged American in Syria when we passed a baked, dusty farm where a man and a boy were ploughing with a primitive hoe. 'The trouble is perfectly obvious,' my companion said, after watching them for a while. 'They're not really working. If they'd put their back into it they'd improve their lot practically overnight. I've seen this all over the place—India, Ceylon, everywhere. These people are reaping just exactly what they sow. They're lazy.'

There seemed to be no point in explaining to him that this particular farmer had spent his life on 1¼ lbs. of poor quality food per day and that he was physically incapable of being as energetic as an American who eats nearly 5 lbs. of well-balanced, nourishing food a day.

In Bombay more than 350,000 men, women and children sleep outdoors because they happen not to possess a roof under which to sleep, so not surprisingly hunger is rife. I remember being shocked the first time I saw a man collapse from hunger in a busy street—and shocked as much by the public's apparently callous indifference as by his hunger. But the people of Bombay are hardened to hunger-collapses; they happen all the time. Hunger is an elementary fact of life unworthy of comment, so most people simply step over or walk around a person who has fallen over in the street. They are not being unfeeling, really; they feel, simply, that there is nothing to be done. Eventually somebody, a policeman perhaps, will drag the man or woman to shelter or send him to hospital—if he is very lucky—and somebody will give him a handful of rice or a chapatti. This will sustain him for a little while until he faints again. Or dies. But Indians cling to life with astonishing tenacity, although nine million of them die each year.

In three hours' walk late one hot night in Calcutta I counted 510 people, men, women and children, sleeping in dirty holes in walls, in doorways, on the streets, under vehicles and bridges, on the tops of parked cars. But 510 was a small proportion of the 600,000 miserable, hopeless wretches of Calcutta who have no roof over their heads.

'These Indian girls are beautiful!' a woman tourist said

during a trip around Karachi. 'So slender, such elegant
shoulders and such big, beautiful eyes. And don't they walk
languidly!' The girls she saw were Pakistanis, but like their
Indian cousins they were slender because they were underfed. Their eyes were big because they dominated the small-
ness of their features. They walked languidly because all
Indians and Pakistanis have learned not to waste the little
energy they have.

A few years ago when famine devastated West Honan,
China, an American reporter, Teddy White of *Time* magazine, wrote one of the most searing accounts of the face of
hunger in its most virulent form—famine. 'My notes tell me
that I am reporting only what I saw or verified; yet even to
me it seems unreal: dogs eating human bodies by the road,
peasants seeking dead human flesh under cover of darkness,
endless deserted villages, beggars swarming at every village
gate, babies abandoned to cry and die on every highway. . . .
Nobody knows or cares how many refugees die on this road.
. . . Of Honan's 34 millions we estimated there have been
three million refugees. In addition, five million will have died
by the time the new harvest is gathered. . . . Trees on the
road have been peeled of their bark. Peasants dry and powder
the elm bark and then cook it. They also eat leaves, straw
roots, cottonseed and water reed. . . . When they die they just
lie down in the slush or gutters and give up. . . .'

Almost every year since 108 B.C. there has been a famine
in some part of China, but famine has an almost universal
and timeless history and even countries in which imagination cannot now conceive a famine have suffered in their day.
Between A.D. 10 and 1846 the British Isles had 201 recorded
famines, the latter date being the year of the great Irish
famine.

Famine and hunger are spreading. Ironically, it is starkly
present in the most prosperous and best fed countries. Even
the United States, with its embarrassing flow of food, has
very hungry people. There is no room for complacency any-

26

where; the so-called 'population explosion', abetted by the hunger problem, will not confine itself to any artificial boundary and sooner or later must have its effect everywhere in the world. This may not happen directly or imminently. It is impossible to imagine that countries like Australia and New Zealand will ever find themselves unable to feed their own people, but they could easily find themselves over-run by the hundreds of millions of hungry people from less fortunate countries, all rebels in the 'revolution of rising expectations'. For this and other reasons to be discussed in this book hunger is a world problem requiring a world solution.

Basically, people have one of two views about food. If they sell it then it is merely another trade commodity, produced and sold for profit according to the natural law of demand and supply. The consumer sees food as an urgent daily necessity and therefore by its very nature not to be treated as an ordinary item of trade. The hungrier a man and his family are the more ardently he looks at food this way.

Responsibility for food supply is no longer a matter for communities or even single countries; it is international and must be so tackled. By failing to tackle it vigorously enough the 'haves' of the world are guilty not merely of criminal negligence but of gross and culpable manslaughter. The very existence of the Food and Agriculture Organization shows some awareness of this fact, but even now the truth is not internationally accepted at general public level.

'Normal' hunger as distant from 'crisis' hunger is an insidious problem, for people will not respond to it in the way that they will respond to a cry for help following an earthquake, volcano or flood disaster. A catastrophe of this kind captures headlines and appeals to public imagination and sympathy. But hunger, being ever-present, and quite unspectacular, arouses no similar feelings. Help for a natural disaster springs from a white heat of emotion and is quite spontaneous; help for hunger needs to be cold-blooded and deliberate.

There is no sight quite so horrifying as that of a small child suffering from malnutrition or starvation. Even a battlefield scene with its torn, broken and dismembered bodies is not so disturbing, for one can at least find some consolation in the reflection that these men are dead and now beyond suffering. In Salonika, I saw a Greek child of about three or four in an advanced state of under-nourishment. His skin was loose in places and around the upper arms hung in folds; his ribs showed starkly through his skin; his knees were knobbly; his head was too large by far in proportion to the rest of his body. Perhaps worst of all, his eyes were dead and his face was that of an old man. If he should live this child will never have known what it was to be a child. If he should live.

Millions of people lack sufficient starchy foods and the consequent calories, and millions more depend on manioc and tapioca, which certainly relieve hunger but do not provide adequate nutriment. When a baby is weaned on a diet inadequate in proteins its stomach swells, its skin cracks like old lacquer and its hair rusts. Lack of Vitamin A can cause blindness—xeropthalmia—and many an infant suffers from dehydration or hunger-toxicosis, from which it will die unless given a transfusion.

Thirty-five million people die of starvation and under-nourishment every year; that is, almost three times the population of Australia or approximately the entire population of Spain. Thirty-five million lives snuffed out of existence. But the tragedy only begins there, for in a way these people are better off than many who manage to survive only to endure the intolerable burden of lifelong hopelessness.

In this era of the mass communication media of press, radio and television it is unbelievable that the wealthier half of the world does not know how the other half lives, so the apparent conclusion is that the one does not *care* how the other lives. Occasionally there is a splutter of over-righteous indignation, or token or even sincere gestures of horror, but they come to little. The clammy veil of complacency clutches, it seems, the whole of the prosperous world.

3   THE MEANING OF POVERTY

Poverty and hunger and over-population are the major problems of the second half of the 20th century. They are going to loom increasingly, frighteningly large as each year ticks away. The trouble is that a man needs to be hungry and poor before he realizes that anybody else might be in the same situation. In some areas very few people are poor and hungry, so we have the paradox that these wealthy people, who have the power to help ease the lot of their under-privileged fellows, will not do so. But if they are themselves to survive they must act before long.

Facts, being stark, speak for themselves—and what follows is fact, not opinion.

Paul Hoffman, of the United Nations Special Fund, has said that 100 major communities, with a total population of 1,500 million, are appallingly poor. The annual income per person is £35, about 100 dollars; this means a weekly living allowance of 75p. In some countries £35 would be regarded as a fairly high income; in India the figure is only £20.

But some authorities say that £70 a year is the 'poverty border'. This figure would take in Asia, Japan, Israel, parts of Eastern Europe, even parts of Western Europe such as Portugal, all of Africa except the Republic of South Africa, most of Latin America and nearly all of Oceania, excluding Australia and New Zealand. These areas collectively hold two-thirds of the human race or about 2,000 million people.

Those who seek to play down the problem say that the oil countries, such as Venezuela, cannot be included in poverty areas because the *per capita* income is high. But here statistics lie. On paper, Venezuela has the highest *per capita* income in Latin America, but a recent president, Mr. Betancourt, admitted that millions of Venezuelans are desperately poor; none of the massive oil income goes into their pockets.

In any case, income expressed in terms of money is a misleading yardstick. What really matters is what the money will buy. Assuming he had the know-how, an Indian or Pakistani could improve his lot a great deal if he owned and could afford to operate a mechanical plough, or if he could buy fertilizer. But a plough would cost him much more than he earns in a lifetime and even fertilizer would cost him a year's income.

There is no reason to suppose that humanity will soon reach the limits of *potential* food production, for the more vigorously we press them the more they recede. But this is theory, for whether man will in fact produce enough food for his needs is problematical and depends on many things, chief of which are the ignorance, unpredictability and sheer cussedness of man himself.

This globe does have sufficient resources to feed its present propulation and a large increase. However, this fact is not so heartening as it might appear, for it is hedged about with so many qualifications and conditions. The resources and potential exist, but they must be made known to countless millions who have no idea of their existence; they must be developed and exploited. And somehow or other the distribution must be made more equitable. Today, only 3 per cent of the land surface of the globe—57 million square miles —is usable for food production. More and more land must be irrigated; spoiled and eroded land must be brought back into use; land at present sound and healthy must not be allowed to deteriorate through erosion or salination; especially must aquaculture be developed more intensively and to a greater extent; people must be educated to appreciate that 'odd' foods can be valuable foods—seaweed for example. And above all food must be more evenly distributed.

Europeans, like Americans, have plenty of reason to feel satisfied for the moment. The European's standard of living is going up and by 1975 he will be living better, making more money and getting better education, despite black spots such as parts of Greece, Spain, southern Italy and Portugal.

In the so-called Western or developed countries a farmer can afford to buy a tractor, a plough and fertilizer. He increases his yield, makes more money and can afford to buy further aids. The blunt fact is that wealth breeds wealth and poverty breeds even more abject poverty, so that the gap between the developed nations and the under-developed nations grows wider by the year, despite all that is being done to put on brakes.

Optimism concerning world food is desirable, but realism cannot be ignored. Therefore, it must be said that it is questionable whether the poorer countries will ever catch up with the richer ones. The fact that the U.S.A. and India had more closely comparable living conditions 150 years ago than they do now is significant.

Figures can certainly be made to lie, but these figures are straightforward enough. The Far East, bolstered by China's massive 800 million people, has 53 per cent of the world's population, but only 12 per cent of the world's income. Africa, 7 per cent of world population, has 2.5 per cent of

THE HUNGER TO COME

income; Latin America has nearly 7 per cent of population, 4.7 per cent of income. North America, with 6.7 per cent worth of people has nearly 40 per cent of income, and Europe, with 22.2 per cent has almost as much income. Australia and New Zealand and the rest of Oceania have a mere 0.5 per cent of total population, but more than 1.5 per cent of income.

Expressed in easily comprehensible form, the 19 richest nations in the world control three-quarters of the world's income—but are peopled by only 16 per cent of the entire population.

The rest of the world suffers from poverty. Poverty is a term which requires some explanation and emphasis in order to make clear the intent and message of this book.

Very few people in the developed nations have any conception of real poverty. Personally, I have not experienced true poverty or hunger, except on active service in wartime, but I have seen it at first-hand in the Middle and Near East, in India and Pakistan and in parts of South-east Asia. Poverty means total lack of amenities. To express it starkly, millions and millions of people have never seen toilet paper or any other hygienic necessity. They have neither soap nor toothbrush. When ill, they are unlikely to see a doctor, if only because in poor countries there is only one doctor for every 50,000 or 75,000 people. No matter how willing he might be, one doctor serving an area of perhaps 15,000 square miles could not reach parts of it under two days and in the rainy season he could not possibly reach many parts.

Poverty can also be revealingly measured by the number of dentists available. At the last count 15 million people living in African countries and territories had 250 trained dentists; five of these countries, with a population of 60 million, had 50 dentists—more than a million people to one dentist. In the United States there is a dentist to every 2,000 people and in Britain one to every 2,200.

Poverty results in parents watching their children die from

32

disease or lack of food. Often the death is a long, wasting one—the worst of all.

Poverty is having an eternally bare cupboard and being in debt to the local moneylender for life.

Poverty means no heating in winter and no cooling in scorching summer; it means one ragged set of clothing, practically no furniture and almost nothing in the cupboard, which in any case does not exist.

The Food and Agriculture Organization, a sober, non-alarmist body, estimates that about one-seventh of the world's population is underfed and consequently suffering from malnutrition, which in turn leads to beri-beri, pellagra, keratomalacia and *kwashiorkor,* among other diseases.

Kwashiorkor—that 'illness of many names'—is traditionally associated with the early weaning that results when pregnancies are closely spaced. A child suffering from the disease —which is the infantile pellagra of South Africa, fatty liver disease or 'sugar baby' of Jamaica, the 'm'buaki' of the Congo, 'nutrition dystrophy' of India and 'distrofia pluricarencial infantile' of South America—is suffering from protein malnutrition. He fails to gain weight, he is peevish, his appetite fails. He has complicated gastro-intestinal infections which many uninformed mothers 'treat' by putting their children on an even more restricted diet, thus aggravating the condition. A curious symptom is body swelling and patchy bleaching of the hair which in some parts of Africa is so common that it is considered a normal stage of development. Children suffering from advanced *kwashiorkor* will die without medical treatment. Those suffering from mild *kwashiorkor* easily fall victim to other diseases and their mental and physical development is endangered.

It is probable that nearly all African children have suffered from *kwashiorkor*. Nutritional anaemia also claims many lives, particularly among expectant mothers. Pellagra is endemic among people subsisting on a maize diet, as so many do in parts of Latin America, Africa and the Near East.

c   33

Real treatment of *kwashiorkor* is simple—a diet of protein-rich skim milk. This cures, in weeks, even gravely ill
children. But many children never get this simple treatment.
The World Health Organization and the F.A.O., with other
United Nations agencies, has helped greatly. F.A.O. has
worked to raise milk consumption throughout the world.
U.N.I.C.E.F. has distributed 1,500,000 lb. of dried skim milk
for child-feeding projects. But in many areas there is not
enough milk or the milk that is available is too expensive
for most families to buy. An extract of soybean is a partial
substitute for milk in China and India. Japan, Thailand, Formosa, Indonesia and the Philippines are experimenting
with soybean and peanut extracts. Other tests, under F.A.O.
and U.N.I.C.E.F. auspices, are in progress in Iraq, Senegal,
Turkey and Egypt, to use rich protein from cottonseed flour.

A doctor in Western Europe might pass his entire career
without ever examining a child suffering from one of the
many forms of malnutrition so common in tropical and sub-
tropical areas. Some of these nutritional disorders, for
example the blindness that results from acute deficiency in
vitamin A, have not been major health problems in temperate regions for several generations. Others, such as rickets
and endemic goitre, have been practically eliminated. The
child in the developing countries may also be confronted with
a bewildering assortment of infections and infestations rang-
ing from the microscopic malarial parasite to a variety of
clearly visible 'worms' such as hookworms, round worms
and tapeworms.

Common childhood epidemic diseases such as measles and
whooping cough, which are generally comparatively harm-
less in the developed countries, claim many young under-
nourished children in the tropics. But the greatest threat
comes from respiratory diseases such as bronchitis and pneu-
monia and from diarrhoeal diseases. The fevers and excessive excretion of nitrogen associated with such ailments lead
to losses of energy and protein greater than the daily intake.

34

There is a steady drain on the body's reserves and the onset of protein-calorie deficiency disease is generally rapid.

Protein-calorie malnutrition, compounded by the lack of good quality food and the loss of essential nutrients caused by disease, is the biggest menace of future health of the nations in the developing regions. Fortunately, the child who is successfully breast-fed is generally safe from malnutrition until the age of about four to six months. This is shown by the fact that during this period of life the increases in height and weight of babies in developing countries parallel those of babies in areas such as North America and Western Europe.

The crisis begins a little later when the mother's milk supply cannot meet even the minimum nutritional needs of the growing child and its diet is supplemented with food of inadequate quality and concentration of calories and good protein. If the breast feeding continues the more dramatic symptoms of malnutrition are largely avoided, although the child's growth may well be retarded. It is when the child is completely weaned, sometimes between the age of one and three years, that the critical period for malnutrition begins.

Weaning comes at a time when the child needs about twice as much protein, in relation to body weight, as do adults. Instead, a child in the tropics and subtropics is likely to be fed a diet rich in starches and poor in protein, vitamins and certain essential mineral elements. In developing countries, where custom prescribes special foods for children of this age, these are generally bland, starchy preparations—based on yams, cassava, bananas, arrowroot, maize, rice gruel and the like—and they are often less nutritious than the foods that the rest of the family eats. Weakened by such meagre fare the child may well fall victim to diarrhoeal and other diseases. The mother frequently blames the child's illness on 'rich foods' and its diet is likely to be further restricted to beverages, such as rice water and tea, and thin gruels all of which contain fewer calories and practically no protein whatsoever. The protein-calorie malnutrition which was already likely to develop now becomes inevitable.

When the child suffers from a severe lack of calories as well as a shortage of proteins, he is really in a state of semi-starvation—euphemistically described as under-nourishment—and the symptoms are different. In this condition, known as *marasmus*, the child becomes little more than skin and bones. *Marasmus* can be distinguished from *kwashiorkor* early in the disease's development by the amount of fat deposited under the skin. Scanty deposits of fat reveal that a child is suffering from both protein and calorie shortages, indicating the likelihood of *marasmus*. In either case the child's future is equally grim unless given the proper remedial care.

Other forms of malnutrition found in children in the developing countries involve shortages of vitamins and essential minerals. Children between the ages of six months and three years, for example, appear to be particularly vulnerable to shortages of vitamin A. One of its most tragic effects is to scar the surface of the eye and, if the deficiency is not corrected in time, the victim becomes completely blind. Rickets, the bone deforming disease caused by a deficiency of vitamin D, is still found in certain areas, even though all that may be required to correct the shortage is sunlight: children in these areas are kept indoors most of the day and protected from the sun when taken outside; 'Sunlight deficient' rickets is particularly prevalent in Moslem countries where sunlight is readily available but social customs prevail against exposing infants to view and fresh air.

Surveys made in developing countries indicate that cases of protein-calorie malnutrition, showing the symptoms described earlier, are found in children of one to nine years with a frequency of between 2 and 10 per cent, being most common between the ages of six months and three years. But the number of children found to be underweight when compared with well-fed, healthy children living in the same community suggests that less extreme forms of malnutrition are very common indeed. In some areas, it is likely that at any one time up to 50 per cent of the children aged one to five years may be in this condition. Surveys in Central America, Colombia, Ghana, India, Ivory Coast, Nigeria, Tunisia and many other countries have shown that the protein and calorie requirements of children are often covered only to the extent of 70 to 80 per cent even though the family, as such, may have adequate and satisfactory diets. This is not due to any unkindness on the part of the father and mother toward their children—far from it—but to an ignorance of the comparatively greater needs of small children for good quality foods.

Less direct evidence for malnutrition comes from the mortality rates of children. Whereas the death rate for live-born children under one year of age is less than 40 per thousand in industrial countries, it is about 100 per thousand in many Asian and Latin American countries and over 200 per thousand in some African countries.

A large number of these children die as a direct consequence of protein-calorie malnutrition, but probably even more die because their resistance to disease is reduced by poor nutrition. They lack the reserves of protein needed to carry them over the period of their illness. In well-nourished people acute disorders have usually run their course before nutritional deficiencies become apparent, but in poorly nourished people the deficiency is immediately significant and malnutrition and infection join forces, often with fatal results. Deaths from respiratory and gastro-intestinal infections, both of which involve serious losses of protein nitrogen, are 20 to 50 times higher in the one-to-four-year age group in developing countries than in industrialized countries. Much of this difference may be attributed to malnutrition.

By the time a child in the developing countries reaches school age he may have escaped from the nutritional 'dark age' of infancy. The twin problems of malnourishment and under-nourishment are not over, but a child of six can adapt to the adult household diet, inadequate though this may be, and make his needs felt. Mild malnutrition may have done little more than leave him smaller in stature than better-fed contempories. If severe malnutrition occurred in the first few months of life, in the womb or after birth, his mental development may have been impaired and his capacity for learning curtailed. In some areas alterations in personality, which still persist after serious malnutrition has been treated, can become so prevalent that they threaten to become part of local cultural characteristics.

Far from being a spur to endeavour, as it was long regarded, chronic hunger is now revealed as a serious impediment to the realization of individual and national goals.

During World War II the British Government carried out extensive tests which showed that when a person's daily intake was less then 2,800 calories a day he started to lose weight. By Western standards, at that time, the British diet was inadequate in quality and quantity. 60 per cent of the world's population have fewer than 2,200 calories per person and half this number have less than 1,900 calories. Only 21 countries—the obvious ones—exceed 2,800 calories.

In a hundred thousand towns and villages in the hunger belt tens of millions of people have never known anything but hunger. This is providing ammunition for the apologists who will say that in this case they cannot be aware of being hungry. In most cases, these people work harder than any Westerner could on the same diet.

The American city-dweller factory-worker eats 4.66 lb. of well-balanced food a day, so he can afford to work hard. The average Indian has 1.23 lb. of food a day, of which 85 per cent is rice. With few proteins, vitamins and fats it is impossible for the Indian either to work hard or live long. Perhaps even more importantly, this lack even deprives the Indian of the *will* to work and live. The apathy, fatalism, melan-

choly and irritability so frequently associated with the
Indian and others is due to his disheartening diet. The rot
goes even further than this. When subjected to prolonged
hunger people can lose all sense of moral values and will
become vicious and unstable.

The average diet figures for Britain and India are significant.

In Britain the average person eats in one year:	The average Indian peasant eats in one year:
20 lb. butter	385 lb. rice
270 pints of milk	
10 lb. margarine	
52 lb. cakes and biscuits	26 lb. pulses (peas, beans,
10 lb. cheese	lentils)
126 lb. bread	
6 lb. lard and compound fats	
20 lb. flour	27 lb. other vegetables
107 lb. meat	
150 lb. potatoes	
39 lb. green vegetables	9 lb. fruit
52 lb. other vegetables	
10 lb. tomatoes	
20 lb. apples	2 lb. fats and oils
16 lb. citrus fruits	
9 lb. other fresh fruit	
18 lb. canned fruit	2 lb. meat
21 lb. poultry	
9 lb. fish	
250 eggs	and less than one pound of
48 lb. sugar	cereals, fish, eggs, milk, sugar.

Lack of quality in the food which the people of the underdeveloped countries eat is as damaging as the lack of adequate quantity. Cereals and starchy foods make up an
unhealthy proportion, rising to as much as 73 per cent in

the Far East, compared with 25 per cent in the U.S.A. and 31 per cent in Britain. Perhaps even more stark is the contrast between what the 'haves' and 'have-nots' eat in the way of milk, meat, eggs and fish: North America 40 per cent, Britain 27 per cent, Africa 11 per cent, the Near East 9 per cent and Far East 5 per cent. Again, grams of protein per person per day range from 92 in North America to 57 in the Far East.

On top of all these troubles, in the underfed countries, 3 million die annually from malaria, though the apologists might find some satisfaction in the fact that another 297 million suffer the disease each year but survive. Another 5 million die of T.B. Millions more suffer or die from trachoma, yaws, leprosy, bilharzia. Active tuberculosis is a concomitant of malnutrition.

In some parts of Africa and Asia almost half the children die before they reach the age of five, while of the approximately 1,000 million children in the world about two-thirds are in need.

Even in one single area great discrepancies occur. For instance, in the Republic of South Africa native life expectancy is 43 years, while white life expectancy is 66 years. But 43 is comparatively long-lived; in Egypt expectation of life is 35 years and in India 32 years.*

To say that in wealthy countries animals are treated better than are humans in poor countries might seem like poetic exaggeration. But it is a fact. About 200 million people live in sub-human conditions and, extraordinarily, 30 million of them come from wealthy countries, such as the United States.

What *is* sub-human? Well, in Lima, Peru, almost one-third of the population lives in '*barrudas*'—settlements of old pieces of wood and sheets of iron. They have one water tap and one toilet to each 100 families and they eat one 'meal' a day. One-third of the population of Rio de Janiero live in

* In England until the 17th century life expectancy was only about 30 years.

the appalling sub-human *'favalles'*—filthy, rotting, slums. Each slum area contains as many as 70,000 people, many of whom live on exposed hillsides with a tap 15 minutes' rough climb away.

In the slums of Santiago, Chile, people live in huts of corn stalks plastered with mud. Many of them die alone and unnoticed by the side of the paths which vein their nauseating slum.

In steaming, opulent Caracas, Venezuela, another 430,000 people live in the 'barrios', existing on whatever they can beg or steal, smothered by squalor and a prey to all the moral vices and physical diseases that abound in such areas. In Beirut, Lebanon, with its seafront façade of luxury hotels, thousands of people live in tin huts and hope when they lie down in their sacks each night that the next day they will somehow find some bread.

The United Nations and the F.A.O. estimates that, to cope with the tremendous expansion of population, cereal production must increase by 100 per cent and animal products by 200 per cent. But this would be no solution to the problem. It would mean merely that instead of about 1,500 million people being inadequately fed more than 3,000 million would be hungry. In other words, the increase in food would only keep pace with population growth. To raise diet to something like an adequate amount, animal products must be increased by well over 300 per cent.

For every 100 million increase in population we will need 13 million more tons of cereals and 14 million tons of meat, milk, eggs and fish. Reduced to more readily comprehensible terms, the Near East will need a cereal increase of 78 per cent and a milk increase of 81 per cent by 1980. If the prosperous peoples of the world think that shortages cannot affect them —by virtue of their efficiency—they are in for a shock. Even in Europe cereals must increase 22 per cent and milk by 45 per cent by 1980.

It would be easy to moralize and point out that the money

spent on space research and defence could have by now ensured sufficient food and water for every person on earth, but since man has no intention of cutting back on space research and defence, we shall have to do the best we can with the financial resources available.

Nevertheless it is true to say that until the richer nations feel that it is more important to spend a few hundred million pounds to conquer hunger and poverty rather than several thousand millions on conquering space, then millions more people will assuredly die of starvation.

It is specious and point-evading to claim that the world could support a vast increase in population. The obvious fact is that it does not support them, so that whether or not it could do so is merely academic quibble. In any case, mere existence, lacking all dignity, is not enough. People must be able to live as human beings, as people, not as human animals. But in order to feed the growing mass of humans at a level above subsistence more than 70 square miles of territory needs to turn over to agriculture every day.

Notestein, a leading authority, has said, 'Only in a society in which the individual child or adult has a reasonable chance for survival in healthy life, will develop that interest in dignity and material well-being essential to the reduction of fertility.'

The revolution of rising expectations is apt to become more violent and persistent, for people in the less fortunate countries are no longer in ignorance about the rest of the world. Their radios and even their TV sets tell them there are worlds of plenty across the seas, and this news makes them discontented and envious.

Pandit Nehru could have been referring to the revolution when he said: 'People think today in terms of social justice. They accept less and less the dictates of "fate" and "*kismet*" —"because I am poor, I must remain poor".'

The 'have-nots' no longer believe, as they once did, in a destiny which decrees that they must live a life of misery, degradation and early death. The extreme imbalance of food and money is building up dangerous tensions in the poorer countries and this tension must reach breaking point. Yet the imbalance increases while the prosperous countries continue to live in a fool's paradise, blind to the dangers to world peace and stability.

Ritchie Calder, that most ardent exponent of food-sense and birth control logic, quotes some significant comment by Ernest Bevin when he was Foreign Secretary. Speaking to an audience of Lancashire housewives, he said: 'You complain because you can't get fish suppers in Lancashire. Why can't you get fish suppers? The Fleetwood trawlers are bringing in the fish and there's plenty of potatoes. But the fish-fryers can't fry. And why can't they fry? Because there's trouble in Indonesia; because there's a lot of bother in Burma and because we haven't got things straightened out in Siam. And because India has to grow more food for its own people, we can't get nuts from India. And because we can't get ground nuts from India the fish fryers can't get the oil. And *you* can't get your fish and chips.'

All countries are dependent on other countries. This is why hunger is not merely somebody else's problem. Things still are not straightened out in Indonesia, Burma, Thailand and India—not by a long way.

4 POPULATION CONTROL AND MIGRATION

The use of the term 'population explosion' has been criticized on the grounds that it is extravagant phraseology, but in fact it is quite apt.* In the long run this explosion will cause just as much damage to the world as any nuclear war. Certainly a technological explosion is taking place, slowly, at the same time, but the resources of the world must reach a limit somewhere, some time, while population expansion appears to have no limit.

We got into this situation because medical science and efficient public health schemes have been able to depress the death rate with remarkable speed and the same time dramatically increase the birth rate. It is all a matter of balance. For thousands of years the birth rate only slightly exceeded the death rate. Now the difference is astonishing. In just 10 years,

* The terms 'population explosion' and 'population bomb' appear to have been first used in a pamphlet issued by the Hugh Moore Fund, U.S., 1954.

1940–50, the death rate declined by 46 per cent in Puerto Rico, 43 per cent in Formosa and 23 per cent in Jamaica.

Some sample differences between the birth and death rates per 1,000 inhabitants per annum.*

Country	Birth Rate	Death Rate
Albania	35.6	8
Australia	20	9.1
Brazil	43	12
Canada	17.7	7.4
Costa Rica	46	9
Egypt	38·2	16.2
Guyana	41	9
India	41.7	22.8
Mauritius	31.4	9.1
Mexico	45	11
Poland	16.3	7.7
United Kingdom	17.1	11.9
United States	17.4	9.6
U.S.S.R.	17.3	7.7

I have already referred to the ultimate misery facing mankind; in many places for many millions of people misery is already here. As for the population explosion, in some areas it is no long-term problem but an immediate and appalling fact. A small country like Mauritius vividly illustrates the problem in its most acute form. Anybody who has been in Mauritius when the children come out of school in the afternoon will appreciate the term 'population explosion'.

Then the streets swarm with children, many of whom will never be able to find jobs. It is said in Mauritius that women have children but no periods; they marry at 15 and from then on are pregnant until the end of their child-bearing lives. I know of one couple who had 16 children, six of whom died.

* United Nations Population Commission Report, July 1970.

45

Most of the others are now married and so far have given their parents 39 grandchildren. Within 45 years—and the grandparents might well live much longer—they could have 500 grandchildren. This one family is representative of many.

For a long time Mauritius managed to amble along on a middle course—her standard of living was low in comparison with Western countries but high compared with many African countries and Indian areas. Before 1939 the population was growing by only one-half per cent per year. Then in 1946-7 malaria was wiped out on the island and the population increase shot up to 3 per cent per year.* The population is now approaching 850,000; by the year 2000 it will be three million—unless family planning is successful.

In 1966 the number of children was already so large that if, from that time, no further births occur on the island the number of people looking for jobs in 1980 would still be 50 per cent greater than it was in 1966.

For hundreds of years Mauritius has been peaceful, but in recent years unrest has become a slow cancer in the island, as frustration and helplessness make themselves felt. The premier frankly admits that nothing he and his government can do will prevent the standard of living from going down, despite the work of birth control advocates and instructors. In Mauritius even the Catholics teach birth control, although by 'natural' methods only.

How are the Mauritians to be fed, let alone assured of a dignified, useful life of labour? The island is 99 per cent dependent on sugar, which can be grown on only a limited

* If preventive medicine were pushed hard in all countries the population explosion would become even more volcanic. This can be seen in microcosm by the experience of the suburbs of Georgetown, Guyana. Due to the extensive use of D.D.T., infant mortality fell, in the years between 1947-9, from 350 to 67 per 1,000 births; in seven years the population doubled and in 1964 it had redoubled. At the present rate of growth Ceylon will more than double its population in about 20 years, largely because the death rate has dropped by more than 60 per cent since 1945.

46

amount of land. Somebody has suggested glibly that 'massive development of new industries might be a partial solution', but Mauritius has had no industrial experience, her raw materials are few and how could she hope, in her geographical isolation, to compete with the experienced trading nations? If ever there were a case for planned, government-fostered birth control, Mauritius provides it.

Colombia provides another, with a population-doubling time of 22 years. About 1947 death control arrived in Colombia. It was a mixed blessing. Before medical technology took a hand in Colombia's problems a woman undergoing 10 pregnancies could expect to have two or three children survive to reproductive age. Now, despite dreadful malnutrition,* medicine keeps about eight children alive. The financial burden is impossible—80 per cent of the family income goes on food—and the mother's despair pathetic. The average mother goes through a progression of attempts to limit her family.† She starts with ineffective native forms of contraception then deteriorates to quack abortion, infanticide, frigidity and, in many cases, to suicide.

Look at some figures. In 1650 the world's population was something like 500 million. By 1900 it was 1,602 million. Sixty years later it had grown to 3,000 million by 1980 it will be 4,457 million and by A.D. 2000 it will be crowded with probably 7,000 million people. This is the sober estimate of the United Nations Population Commission.

Looking beyond A.D. 2000 the problem becomes staggering. About 2050 the population will be 15,000 million, a century later 82,000 million and by 2350 a frightening 440,000 million will be reached. Perhaps 'would be' is a better term, for many demographers estimate that, with present knowledge, the world can support a maximum of

* Arthur Hopcroft, travelling the world on hunger research in 1967, reported 100 infant deaths a day from malnutrition.

† The research of Dr. Sumner Kalman, Professor of Pharmacology, Stanford University School of Medicine, speaking to the Palo Alto Kiwanis Club, January 25, 1968.

30,000 million people. Admittedly, 300 years is too long a period to forecast, but the figures do indicate the gravity of the problem.

Look at it this way: the human race took 200,000 years to reach its present figure, which will be doubled by the end of the century.

The peoples of the developed countries are living in a fool's paradise. How many of them have given thought to the implications of the fact that by 1982 one in four of the world's population will be Chinese? Or that by the end of the century 75 per cent of the total population will be clustered in the underdeveloped countries?

The die-hards, fighting a fierce rearguard action against birth control, like to point out that there is no global overpopulation. One has referred to New York with its 22,000 people per square mile enjoying a high standard of living. The same writer, using figures for his own ends, shows that Monaco has a population density equal to 40,000 per square mile, also with a high standard of living. He could have made out a better case for casuistry had he got his figures right: in fact, Monaco has a population density of 42,500 to the square mile. But the writer was being deliberately and crudely misleading. He did not bother to point out that Monaco covers an area of only 370 acres and that the total population, at the time, was 22,297. It is now 23,000.

The luxury living enjoyed by these few would hardly console the 40,000 people of Cairo who have nowhere to sleep but the streets. Some writers prove, at least to their own satisfaction, that the world as a whole is not menaced by population explosion. The phrase 'as a whole' is theirs, and in it lies the whole weakness of their argument. It is obvious that if only two countries—Australia and Canada, for example —are not facing over-population then the world 'as a whole' is not doing so. But again, the Indians, Pakistanis, Chinese and many others would view the argument with bitter cynicism. They are not concerned with 'the world as a whole', but with their own existence.*

Another not-so-white lie claims that the average family has enough to eat. There is no such thing as an average family —in Britain, China, Fiji or anywhere else. The term is a convenient garbage bin for some statisticians. They tot up the total amount of food produced by a country, add it to the total food imports and divide by the number of people in the population. The result is false. Even in the poor countries some families eat very well indeed: families of the military and armed forces eat better than most; the plagues of officials do quite well. The net result is that a vast number of families eat and possess much *less* than 'the average family'.

The professedly unalarmed people have an answer to most of the over-population and hunger fears. They say, for instance, that the population boom is partly due to the rise in life expectancy in most of the world and that when this trend slows and finally stops the gap between births and deaths will be closed. Also, that as the number of people of parenthood age decreases marriage rates and birth rates will begin to fall. They even go so far as to advocate an *increase* in the birth rate. Two writers in the *Catholic Digest* claim that, 'In Europe and the United States there is serious danger that unless the birth rate is raised we shall be living in old-age asylums.'

Several religions show a liberal attitude to birth control; this is specially true of Islam, Hinduism and the Protestant form of Christianity. Where there is little or no Catholic influence the American and Anglo-Saxon attitudes generally are effective. In Asia, this applies to Formosa, Hong Kong, Ceylon, Thailand, Malaya, Singapore and Pakistan.

I am surprised that the 'let's not take all this too seriously'

* Percentage increase in total population between 1960 and 1970: Latin America 29; North Africa 26; South Asia 22; Far East 21; Africa (south of the Sahara) 16; Australia and New Zealand 15; U.S.A. and Canada 14; North Europe 7; European Economic Community 7.

brigade has not used Ireland as an example of lack of population pressure. This is probably because Ireland, being the most notable exception, proves the rule. She is, in fact, the only country of any size which has fewer inhabitants than, say, 150 years ago.

To forestall the criticism that figures are often exaggerated, I should point out that most demographers tend to under-estimate rather than over-estimate. Proof: in 1946 many American demographers* predicted that by 1960 the American population would reach 153 million and 164.5 million about 1990. In fact, this latter figure was reached in 1955—35 years earlier than forecast. By 1975 the figure will approach 228 million.

Of course, much of the discussion about the 'population explosion' is speculative, since it depends on the clause 'if the present birth rate continues'. In the United States, where there is acute anxiety about population figures, the rate has never been stable. In 1800, when the nation needed more children, the fertility rate was about 275 babies per 1,000 women of child-bearing age. In the depression year of 1936 it was as low as 76. In 1957 it reached 123, the highest figure for 40 years. It has since dropped to about 105. The total number of babies born in the United States in 1964— 4,054,000 of them—was the smallest number for 10 years.

In a country of the United States' point of evolution the fertility rate reflects individual decisions, which tended to be influenced by external conditions. As circumstances change so will attitudes about having children, and it seems to me that the United States need not worry about having too many people to support, if only for the realistic reason that birth control techniques are so widely accepted and practised.

The United States is not having a population explosion in

* The Americans are acutely conscious of the population problem—so much so that they have a Population Association, a society of several hundred scholars all actively engaged in population study. The association even publishes a quarterly review which annually takes note of more than 2,000 references.

the way that China, India, Pakistan, Indonesia and other countries are having it. Paradoxically, there is more open space in the United States now than at any time since the late 19th century—and this with 204 million people. There is more land now classed as 'forest and woodland, not grazed', than for a great many years. This is partly because of the drift to the cities or to certain states. In fact, about half the American population lives on only 1 per cent of the land.

The present density of the American population is only 56 to the square mile. Holland has a density of 940, yet there is much open land in Holland, and it is still as much an agricultural country as an industrial one. West Germany has a density of 610, Japan 685, Great Britain 605, Italy 439 and even 'wide open Switzerland'—as one travel writer describes it—has a density of 377 to the square mile.

The United States could support a population of a thousand million and still have a density of less than 300 to the square mile. However, comforting though this may be to some people, all Americans will have to ask themselves whether they want so many people in their country. Will such a number stifle and impede rather than assist the country's attempts to remain the leader of the 'free world'? All developed countries must sooner or later face the same question, and the present is a good time to begin thinking up an answer. As time goes on many more people will live longer and it is possible that they will create an intolerable burden for any nation's economy.

Some writers are labelled pessimists—but the example of the British Isles has already shown that pessimistic forecast have come true. In the middle of the 19th century, with a population of 20 million, the British Isles were more or less self-supporting, but farsighted people were already warning of shortages. As the population increased home-produced food became inadequate in quantity, and in Ireland population pressure was only relieved by mass emigration to

51

America. Britain exists by being able to sell goods abroad, the money from which she uses to buy food. And, fortunately, there is continuous migration, thus easing the burden. The export of people and of manufactures is all very well as long as other countries are prepared to receive them. Should something happen to upset this balance, Britain, in company with several other countries, will be in a desperate situation. She has, in fact, already been in such a situation.

Over-population faces Britain, though perhaps not so urgently as in some other countries. However, there is no denying that England is the second most crowded country in Europe and that the British birth rate is such that by 1985 there will be eight million more people in England and Wales than in 1965 even taking into account the exodus of emigrants. Even by 1980 a fifth of the population of England will be old-age pensioners—that is, men over 65 and women over 60.

No matter how great are the various schemes for increasing and diversifying food production, there is a limit—fortunately still a long way off—to the quantity that can be produced. Most food experts agree on this point. But there is no apparent limit to population. Few scientists will commit themselves to an optimum figure for world population, but many have explained at length what the consequences of certain numbers would be. Some are even honest and frank enough—as is N. W. Pirie—to point out that probably many more babies are born than are positively wanted by their parents and that this would not happen if contraceptive techniques were more efficient. Unintended or 'casual' births throw a burden on humanity.

In 1798 and again in 1803 Thomas Malthus published his controversial theory that multiplication of people tends to occur in a 'geometric ratio'; that is, the more people there are, the more children they will produce. He estimated that, without any check, human population tended to double every 25 years. Thus, Malthus said, 'the power of population is indefinitely greater than the power of the earth to produce subsistence for man'. He based this hard statement on his theory that the means of subsistence can be increased only at an 'arithmetic ratio'; in short, it could not possibly double every 25 years. Constant improvements in all the facets of farming and food techniques might result in an arithmetic 'run' such as 1, 2, 3, 4, 5. But the population would start from 1, double to 2, then 4, 8, 16, 32—and every schoolboy knows what sort of figure is to be reached by continuing the sequence.

The 'doubling time'—the period necessary for doubling the world's population—seems to be about 34 years at present.* Suppose that the population continued to double every 35 years for 900 years—a ridiculous assumption, perhaps, but the simple mathematical calculation is sobering. The earth would have something like 60 million billion people—100 people for each square yard of the earth's surface, land and sea. A British physicist, J. H. Fremlin,† has calculated that such a multitude might be housed in a continuous 2,000-story building covering the entire planet, with the upper 1,000 stories containing the equipment to operate the immense labyrinth. Half of the space in the bottom 1,000 stories would be needed for pipes, wires, elevator shafts and passages. People would have a maximum of four square yards of floor space. Such calculations are scientifically sound and within the period of 900 years technology will probably have found a way of putting into practice the necessary structures. Where the food will come from no 20th century expert can suggest.

Much of what Malthus wrote still holds good, but few experts now agree entirely with him and it seems quite likely that his geometric-arithmetic ratios could well be dis-

* With significant local variations. The doubling time for Brazil is 22 years; Philippines and Costa Rica, 20 years; El Salvador, 19 years. Longer doubling times are U.S., 63 years; United Kingdom, 140 years; Soviet Union, 63 years.

† In *New Scientist*, October 29, 1964.

rupted even more than they have been already. Still, the great surge of discussion, controversy and thought which followed the publication of his doctrine certainly began the birth control movement as such, even though the practice had been known for centuries. He was also the founder of an incredibly vast literature on population theory and study.

Nevertheless, Malthus could point to case histories since his time to support his own arguments. He could, today, refer to the Irish population as a classic illustration of his theory that population tends to expand to the limit of its food growth. This growth reached 8,175,000 in 1841, before the potato famine gradually halved it.

The problem of artificially controlling population is fraught with difficulties and in some countries a generation must elapse before such a campaign could make any appreciable difference, but it is better to do something now than to talk about plans for the future.* Opponents of the idea raise all sorts of barriers, some valid, some vacuous. One writer says that officially endorsed contraception may give the impression that the pace of economic and social progress is unable to cope with the expected population growth. This, of course, is exactly the situation and it should be admitted and openly stressed, not evaded. Birth control will not solve the problem of over-population and hunger, but it could help to give the world more breathing space.

Widespread birth control seems to me to be the best short- and middle-term method of at least ensuring a continuation of a subsistence diet for the present population.

A long-term measure follows naturally on primary and intermediate birth control. It is axiomatic, if paradoxical, that people who are well fed and confident of security have fewer children. If remedial birth control is efficient and

* The belief that conventional wars influence population is false. During World War II about 30 million people—at the most—lost their lives as a result of the war. This is about six months' increase of world population.

people like the Indians can become well fed and secure then they will, of their own volition, *want* fewer children—at least in principle. Unfortunately, contraceptive practices are closely linked with education and financial status. The birth rate falls with the rise in the standard of living and the expansion of better education. The intellectuals and those with enough money use contraception, but surveys show that the very poor never use it. The deduction is that a long propaganda and publicity campaign is necessary to implant the idea of contraception, followed by free methods of achieving it. Governments of such countries as India might find money spent on contraception campaigns indirectly as fruitful as that spent on irrigation projects. Many an Indian girl dies, worn out from child bearing, at the age of 17. The average age for a girl to marry in many areas is 12, despite an act which fixes the minimum age at 14. In the name of sweet reason, how can any Christian religion object to birth control when such things happen?

The problem of inducing people who have not enough money to buy food, or who receive no wages, to spend what little they have on contraceptives is formidable. This financial obstacle and the other difficulties prevail in three-quarters of the world.

However, some countries seem to have found solutions or partial solutions. In 1939 Puerto Rico was one of the first countries to introduce a birth control programme. It was only mildly successful and the birth rate remained high until 1956 when, quite without official planning, women in large numbers began to have themselves sterilized. In one recent year it was estimated that about 20 per cent of women having babies in hospitals were being sterilized.

Japan's legalized abortion campaign, introduced in the 1950s, has been attacked on moral and religious grounds and has been criticized as ineffective—but not by the Japanese. The Japanese government realized that the soaring birth rate in a country with little space, few raw materials, healthy but inadequate agriculture and ambitious industrial plans could wreck the country's prosperity. In the first 12 months after abortion was legalized 200,000 women made use of it, stark enough proof that many pregnancies were unwanted. By 1955 the figure had grown to 1,200,000 women, almost equal to the number of babies being born each year. In short, Japan succeeded in halving her birth rate when that of most Asian countries was climbing even higher.

In India religious scruples against birth control have almost gone and women in some areas are actually pleading for birth control assistance. Even so, many family planners in India have met with so much frustration and exasperation that they regard family planning a rather grim joke. They persist with it in the belief that in India persistence is necessary to success and because they cannot think of another remedy. The same situation applies in a score of countries.

At the invitation of the Indian government, the United Nations sent a team of experts to India to advise on problems of over-population, especially on the best ways of stepping up birth control campaigns. Led by the secretary-general of the International Planned Parenthood Association, the team advised the Indian government to sterilize husbands over 30 willing to have the operation; to extend the birth control campaign to persuade women to have the plastic coil fitted; to ensure wider distribution of other methods of contraception, including the sheath. The Indian government has even offered payment to husbands who agreed to submit themselves to sterilization, while women's organizations have sponsored contraceptive educational programmes.

Sterilization, especially in countries of low education level, is not the answer. One writer* has estimated that, even if all eligible Indian males could be rounded up, it

* A. S. Parkes, *New Scientist*, July 27, 1967.

would take 1,000 surgeons operating eight hours a day, five days a week a full eight years to sterilize adult Indian males. It would, in effect, be an endless task, for the numbers of Indian males are growing rapidly.

Professor Homi J. Bhabba, an Indian scientist with a world-wide reputation, has suggested that in India's case some fertility-impairing drug should be introduced into public drinking water to help make birth control effective. He would do this only for certain periods of time, so as to gain a 33 per cent reduction in the birth rate. Of course, the suggestion caused an hysterical outburst of protest, but sooner or later politicians will be forced to grasp this nettle.

India is probably the best example of the wide gulf between theory and practice or what-could-be and what-actually-is. Some anti-contraceptionists say that theoretically India could support her present population. Here is even more ammunition for them: Holland with only 0.2 arable acres per person supports a population density more than three times that of India and manages to export food as well. But theory and practice are as far apart as Holland and India are geographically.

I cannot be concerned in this book with a discussion about methods of contraception. However, the two most efficient ways so far devised are the plastic coil and the pill. Occasional scares occur about possible harmful effects of the pill, but at the moment the great weight of medical opinion supports it as the ideal method of making a woman safe from unwanted pregnancy. The plastic coil is slightly less efficient, but it is cheap to produce in quantity, and cheapness is paramount if mass birth control is to succeed in Africa and Asia.

It is important too that medical workers other than doctors should be able to fit the coil, for there are simply not enough doctors to do all the fitting necessary in India, Pakistan, China and many other countries.

The anti-contraceptionists are often advocates of mass

migration. I am not in favour of the developed countries protecting themselves too rigidly with immigration barriers, but to be fair, lowering of barriers would achieve little. After all, the total of all the immigrants who flocked into the Americas, Africa and Oceania during the 19th century and the first part of the 20th century—when barriers did not exist—was less than the present annual increase of world population.

Australia is often criticized for her white Australia policy. Ill-informed critics point to her area of nearly three million square miles and claim that she could support many more than her present 12,550,000. In fact, short of some scheme fabulous enough to open up her arid centre, Australia could support a maximum of 30 million—that is, she could take in about four months' world population increase—a mere drop in the bucket. North Australia might, over a long period, absorb a number of people equivalent to the number of people born in India or China over a period of a few months or a few weeks.

It might be as well to explain briefly here that in reality there is no white Australia policy. The Australian Migration Act makes no distinction between an Asian or a 'white' person. Under this act, an alien is defined as a person who is not a British subject, an Irish citizen or a protected person. Asians are permitted to enter Australia and are doing so in increasing numbers. Many Asian scientists and educationists are employed in Australian universities and colleges. More and more Asian stores and restaurants are being established throughout Australia and all employ Asian labour.

Australia has been accused of a white Australia policy because she has insisted that Asian students return to their native lands on completion of their studies. The students went to Australia intending to learn as much as they could about the skills and techniques of the West so that they might return and help in the urgent development of their own

58

countries; to permit them to remain in Australia would be to defeat the object in view. Many Asians who first entered Australia on temporary permits have, after a time, been permitted to remain and to become naturalized Australian subjects. It is far easier for Asians to enter Australia than it is for them to enter any Asian country other than their own.

The mass movement of people from their own country to another is no solution to the hunger and population problems and would lead to other problems. Population movement is best left to the free will of individuals.

It is sheer ignorance or innocence that leads some people to talk of 'spreading' the world's population more evenly over the globe. Very little spreading can be done, for most people congregate where natural and other conditions most easily provide a means of earning a livelihood and they are not tempted into those areas where living is difficult. Relief, climate, vegetation and accessibility limit the distribution of population, which, far from spreading, has tended in the 20th century to become more concentrated in towns and cities.

The tundra is too cold and remote and is inhabited only by scattered nomads; forest regions naturally impose limits on settlement and are inhabited as a rule only by scattered groups, some of whom are half-civilized; hot deserts, apart from isolated pockets or strips, have few people; mountains are scantily peopled because of ruggedness, severe or uncomfortable climate, poor communications and agricultural limitations. Mountains also have population pockets, often built near the places where minerals have been located, but no 'spreading' can take place. Inaccessible plateaux, such as Tibet, have few people and will always have few people.

The advocates of 'spreading' might as well concede that the idea is not merely dying but dead. People are living in settlements which are becoming more and more concentrated by the year. Even in Australia, where there is certainly room to spread, the drift—or race—to the cities has caused large areas of homes to be razed to make room for tall buildings for mass habitation. The only spreading taking place is upwards, and this is likely to be the trend for many years.

Purely economic migration is rapidly becoming impossible, as France discovered. She tried to induce some of the people of Réunion to move to Madagascar and from the Antilles islands to Guiana, but encountered many insurmountable difficulties.

In any case, the advocates of mass migration have apparently never considered how they would transport their emigrants. To find the ships to carry even four million people would be an impossible task. Every ship and boat in Indian and Asian waters running a shuttle service for a year would make little impression. The mass migration idea is merely a ridiculous substitute for birth control.

Birth control—systematic and on a large scale—must come and it must become international. Those who try to stop it are merely delaying the inevitable and are doing a disservice to humanity and posterity. The time may well come when birth control will have to be enforced by law. This is a distasteful idea, but I find it less revolting than the reflection that so many Mauritians and others have been born into a life of utter degradation, hopelessness, hunger and poverty.

One of the most sobering reflections on the people explosion is that, in 1970, rather more than 40 per cent of the population of the undeveloped world was made up of people under 15 years of age. As they reach reproductive years the population bomb will really go off with a bang.

As Paul Ehrlich has pointed out, there are only two basic solutions to the population problem. One is a 'birth rate solution' in which *we find* ways to lower the birth rate; the other is a 'death rate solution' in which ways to raise the death rate *find us*, in the shape of war, famine and pestilence. Unfortunately, the chance we had of exercising population control has now gone; we have already lost that fight.

Feeding the world's people is only one of two great problems associated with indiscriminate breeding. The other is finding work for them. Urging the need for a world employment program, David Morse, Director-General of the International Labour Office, points to two harsh facts underlying this need:

Economic progress in developing countries though perceptible, is slow; the gap between poor and rich gets wider every day.

The population explosion in these countries impedes progress, and in most of them more than half of the benefits of increased production is absorbed in merely maintaining existing levels of living, low as they are, for ever more people.

Opportunities for work have not increased as fast as the numbers of workers. Scores of millions are entirely bypassed by economic development. And the prospect for the future is even more grim.

During the 1960–70 decade the labour force increased by about 20 million per year and during the next decade it is expected to grow by about 28 million a year. Between 1970 and 1980 more than 280 million people will be added to the world's labour force, 226 million in the less developed regions of the world and 56 million in the more developed regions.

Of these 280 million and more, about 173 million will be added to the labour force in Asia, 32 million in Africa, 29 million in Latin America, 18 million in the Soviet Union, 17 million in North America, 12 million in Europe and 1.3 million in Oceania. The net increase in the world's labour force under the age of 25 will amount to 68 million workers, nearly all of whom (64.5 million) will be added to the labour force of the less developed regions of the world.

The aim of the World Employment Program is to reverse the trend towards ever-growing masses of peasants and slum dwellers who have no part in development. It will do so partly by providing them with the skills needed for productive work and partly through measures of rural development, industrialization, youth employment schemes, investment and international trade. These will enable developing countries to use more of their human resources, and so achieve the prime object of development which, after all, is to bring about a better life for the people.

The World Employment Program is one of the I.L.O.'s principal tasks for the 1970s. It must be an *employment* program because the only path to a better life in the poorer countries is productive work by the people themselves. And it must be a *world* program because, while the main burden will be on the developing countries, the Program cannot succeed without help from the industrialized nations—individually through bilateral programs and collectively through the I.L.O. and other international organizations.

Moreover, the industrialized nations are themselves faced with some difficult employment problems which may also come within the scope of the World Employment Program.

That the majority of urban unemployed should be under 25 years of age, many of them school leavers, is perhaps the most pathetic side of the picture. The problem of unemployment in developing countries is above all the problem of youth. Possible conflicts between maximum employment and maximum production are more complicated than might be supposed. For example, assume a case in which £100,000 is available to increase textile production. If it is invested in a modern textile factory it could produce an extra output of say £40,000 and 100 new jobs. Alternatively the sum could be invested in handspinning and weaving which would produce an output of only £20,000 but 1,000 extra jobs. The conflict between getting maximum output for capital and getting maximum employment out of it is in this case dramatic enough to illustrate the dilemma of choosing between labour-intensive and capital-intensive technologies in development policy.

The creation of employment without economic growth would be as self-defeating as economic growth without the creation of employment. The balance between the two which will prove most advantageous in the long-term is difficult to achieve in practice.

5 WHAT IS BEING DONE AND WHAT COULD BE DONE

Complex and varied reasons underly the lag in food production. One of the most important and direct is the misuse of natural resources, discussed in more detail elsewhere. Destructive agricultural practices have reduced once-fertile areas to wastelands. Perhaps the most blatant of these practices has been the stripping of the earth of its natural cover, thus exposing it to erosion by water and wind. Such practices still continue, partly from ignorance, partly from conservatism, partly because man is intent on producing food for immediate use without any thought for the needs of the future. Inefficiency, too, is rife, but this is not always the farmer's fault. Many a farmer would like to be able to use modern methods and equipment, but cannot possibly afford to do so.

With the hardest work of which he is capable, a peasant farmer can produce enough food for perhaps five people. A Canadian or Australian farmer can produce enough for

475 people. Fed as well as the Canadian or Australian, given the same tools and training, the peasant farmer could learn to be much more productive.

More than 50 per cent of the exports from 26 hungry countries come from a single crop; for instance, Colombia is 75 per cent dependent on coffee. This is dangerous, for when synthetic coffee takes hold—as it will sooner or later—Colombia will be bankrupt. Brazil was in much the same position with her coffee crop, but she has succeeded in diversifying her industries and has even destroyed more than 2,000 million coffee trees and turned the land over to other crops.

Wars have a damaging effect on production, and World War II was particularly disastrous. Food supplies immediately after the war were inadequate everywhere except in North America, Australia and New Zealand and in a few isolated other parts. In Western Europe, the U.S.S.R. and North Africa, agricultural production fell by a third, and in the Far East, where it was already low, it fell by 10 per cent. In some places conditions worsened before they improved; even by 1950 some countries were 20 per cent below normal.

After the war the Food and Agriculture Organization came into being and it is to this body that much of humanity's faith must be pinned. The organization's activities are broad, concerned as they are with all the earth's natural resources, with land, water, farms, forests, crops, trees, animals and fish. It is involved with every aspect of food and agriculture right through to marketing and distribution of food products.

The work of the F.A.O. and especially of its field agents receives little publicity but their work could more radically affect world stability than any effort by politicians. There is not one condition of soil or climate in which these men have not carried out practical schemes of research and education. They have shown the importance of soil conserva-

E   65

tion, irrigation, fertilization, pesticides, machinery and better tools, improved types of seeds, more efficient animal management, prevention of animal and plant disease, human nutrition and hygiene. But all their work needs to be multiplied a hundredfold if it is to make inroads into vast areas of backwardness, for there is no denying the hard fact that in the West less than 15 per cent of the working population produces food in embarrassing excess, while elsewhere 30 per cent of the workforce cannot produce enough food. Up to this point the problem is serious enough, but aggravating it is the great disparity in the density of population and its effect on the availability of land. And on top of this is the uneven productivity of the land.

Throughout the world various programs directed by the F.A.O. and U.N. agencies have many thousands of experts working with governments and counterpart personnel from the recipient countries. More than 90 countries provide the money, and men and women of 66 different nationalities are at work, but the overall task is too gigantic even for money, talent and endeavour on this scale.

In 1970 F.A.O. introduced its Indicative World Plan for agricultural development. The Plan has two vital aims: to show how agricultural production can be made to increase faster than the rate of population growth and to show the scale of effort needed to ensure that all the undernourished millions born and to be born are adequately fed by helping them to increase their own agricultural capacity. They need technical advice and assistance, machinery, equipment and supples on a scale as yet scarcely dreamed of to enable them to achieve such an increase.

The rising curve of world population indicates the need for more capital and human investment in agriculture as well as in industry, more production of raw materials, more and freer international trade and more food. To maintain present nutritional levels food production will have to be increased by about 150 per cent by the end of the century.

If the present rise in world food production of 3 per cent per annum is maintained but not increased, there will still be a gap of some 50-60 per cent in the food needs of the people of the world in A.D. 2000. That is the measure of the need for aid—bilateral and multilateral—and that is the measure of the importance of the Indicative World Plan.

The size of the task may be judged from the fact that if there is to be a fully adequate nutritional level in all countries by the year 2000, the production of milk, meat, eggs and fish must be stepped up to 300 per cent or more over the present output. To achieve the adequate output the U.S. President's Science Advisory Committee has estimated that 124,000 trained men and women will be needed.

The Director-General of F.A.O., Addeke Boerma, recognizes that private industry has a vital role in food supply. 'Whether in the manufacture of production requisites such as fertilizers, pesticides and farm equipment or in the processing of food and other agricultural products in the developing countries, there is enormous scope for mobilizing the managerial abilities, scientific experience and capital resources of private industry.'*

In the hope of mobilizing this powerful source of energy and imagination F.A.O. in 1965 was the first United Nations agency to form a direct link with major industries interested in investing in developing countries. The F.A.O./Industry Cooperative Program is a joint effort to establish industries that are allied to agriculture, forestry and fisheries. F.A.O.'s role in this undertaking is to provide an intelligence service that informs industries of investment needs and opportunities while trying to help governments to contact with foreign enterprises seeking investment openings.

Some developing countries oppose the entry of private capital on principle. Others place stringent restrictions on foreign corporations. But governments endeavouring to attract private capital must recognize that corporations will

* Writing in *Newsweek*'s Global Food Report, August 1968.

not be interested unless a favourable climate exists for investment.

The agribusiness group of companies which are participants in the F.A.O./Industry Cooperative Program have shown an active interest in the whole problem. These companies, which deal in fertilizers, agricultural chemicals, tractors and implements, seeds, irrigation equipment, and the processing of food and forest products, are benefiting both themselves and the cause of development by extending their operations to the less industrialized areas of the world.

Private industry can make an equally significant contribution to two priority programs on which F.A.O. is concentrating its attention—production of protein-rich food and a reduction of the waste of existing sources.

The best advisers come from an underdeveloped country itself, because only they can fully understand the complex social, religious, intellectual and political problems. However, these men must first be trained by overseas experts before going out on their missionary duties.

These experts realize what many other people do not—that the prosperity and success of any country is founded on a rural population successful because of mature agriculture. This takes time, but the foundations so built are much stronger than an economy based on other activities. The truth of this can be seen in any industrial country with a high standard of living—Britain, the U.S.A., Australia, West Germany, Holland, Japan. Here and elsewhere the land has provided the initial wealth and incentive. When more money is paid into farmers' bank accounts than is withdrawn from consumers' accounts, any country's economy improves. Perhaps more important, at least in the long-term, a country farmed as well as it is fed tends to remain much more stable politically.

Countries fall, roughly, into four main food groups.

Group I: U.S.A., Canada, Australia, Argentina, New Zealand, Republic of South Africa. Plenty of food for their own population and much for export.

Group II: Many African countries, the U.S.S.R., most countries of South-east Asia and of Latin America. Could produce all the food they need for home consumption but for various reasons do not.

Group III: Japan, Great Britain, West Germany, Switzerland, Sweden, Denmark and others. Able to produce part of their own food and able to pay for the rest of it, which they import.

Group IV: India, Pakistan, China, Egypt, Iraq. Insufficient local food and no present prospect of paying for the massive imports necessary.

All countries would like to achieve independence in food but this is an improbable ideal in most areas. Australia, with its great climatic range, is one of the few countries to approach the ideal, though others have tried. Malaya's Trans-Perak River Irrigation Scheme is one of the more ambitious plans, particularly in view of the climatic and vegetation difficulties. The scheme covers 180,000 acres of what was formerly tropical jungle and swamp. Its main artery is an 11-mile canal leading from the Perak River, and its veins are four distributory canals. Rice is grown here, as in the other 200,000 acres of new pādi fields. With the relatively low population of 9 million, Malaya, unlike other countries, is in a position to strive for food independence.

Most regions have an acutely imperfect food balance. Tropical Africa illustrates one aspect of this imbalance. The region supplies two-thirds of the world's cocoa, three-quarters of its palm kernels and about 25 per cent of its coffee. Yet the continent as a whole produces only about 6 per cent of world agricultural output. Even the 6 per cent is mis-

69

leading, for it is distributed unevenly, just as Africa's minerals are.

Another factor illustrating imbalance is that in most parts of the world animals are not fed to their full producing capacity. One main reason is that little is done to store surplus grass when it is abundant. Efficient management of pastures backed by some supplementary feeding would greatly increase production—certainly far beyond the quantities of livestock feed used. Millions of farmers must be taught that animals and birds will only give a return in meat, milk and eggs if they are fed above mere existence level.

Japanese productivity and agricultural diversity is an object lesson to the world. Six-sevenths of Japan's total area cannot be cultivated and though there are about 4,000 Japanese to each square mile of arable land—easily the highest proportion in the world—Japan imports less than a quarter of her food supplies, though her population is nearly 100 million. No scrap of land is ignored—even around the base of telegraph posts or on triangles formed by the convergence of roads—all are planted. The Japanese have no fences, and the small foot-wide banks of earth separating the fields are planted with vegetables, usually beans or peas. The Japanese farmers' gardens are so carefully tended that a weed is rarely seen.

Farms are small, averaging only $2\frac{1}{2}$ acres (the average English farm is 100 acres) and the work is very hard, but the Japanese farmer does have something to sell, the heavy urban concentration of industrial workers have the money to pay, and consequently the Japanese farmer can buy fertilizer to increase the quality of his fields, already fertile from water control (no erosion losses), silt brought in by water, and long use of excreta and compost.

By skilled crop rotation and careful manuring the Japanese farmer can grow two crops in the same field in the same year; often the second crop is sown before the first has been harvested. Barley and wheat, for instance, are usually planted in drills and a few months before the grain crop ripens the farmer will sow a crop like tomatoes between the drills. The grain crop is cut by hand to avoid injury to the tomato seedlings. When the barley or wheat has been lifted the drills are split and the tomatoes are off to a flying start.

Small, compact and highly efficient threshing and winnowing machines and ploughs are commonplace in Japan. As there is scarcely anywhere in Japan without electricity the farmers use power for many purposes, including farm machines.

One F.A.O. officer, Dr. Hambridge, has said that if Japanese-type intensive agriculture were practised in East and South-east Asia the result would be a fantastic surplus production of food and a resulting increase in the standard of living.

In the meantime the countries which can feed the world are the U.S.A., Canada, Australia, New Zealand, perhaps those of Europe and possibly Argentina and the Republic of South Africa. These countries not only have the space; they have the capital and skill. Their natural markets are the much poorer countries with rapidly growing populations, but these countries can afford to buy foodstuffs only if the developed countries buy their manufactures, tropical foods and raw materials. In short, by helping the developing countries the advanced countries would be helping themselves.

Despite the undoubted ability of some countries to produce a lot of food, many misconceptions exist about land use and its potential. For instance, there is a widespread belief that Canada, while growing much food, could grow a lot more by putting larger areas under the plough. In fact, only 5 per cent of Canada has ideal or even reasonable conditions for farming.* With her present farming techniques —which are already highly advanced—Canada could not

* India has 40 per cent of her total area under crops, Pakistan and Ceylon 20–25 per cent.

hope to feed more than, say, 30 million people.

The people who want to see vast areas transformed into high-producing agricultural areas sometimes do not look beyond the statistics. Much of most countries is unsuitable because mountain areas are too rugged and have soil too poor to be brought into use without great difficulty. Temperature and rainfall, either too high or too low, eliminate other regions. Areas of dense tropical forest, which at present can be removed only at great expense, are also out.

The majority of people, accustomed to only one type of landscape, apply it to other countries and get a very wrong impression. The British are very prone to do this, for nearly 25 per cent of Britain is arable land and a lot of the rest is grazing land. But other countries are not so fortunate. Only 1 per cent of Australia is crop-land and 2 per cent of Brazil; only 10 per cent of China is intensively farmed. The Amazon region of Brazil covers well over a million square miles; about 200 square miles are cultivated.

The areas under cultivation in the temperate zone of the northern hemisphere and the heavily populated countries of East and South Asia cannot readily be increased, but other places have great agricultural potential. Perhaps the most promising scope lies in the hot, wet equatorial belt, mostly jungle in which a few tribes practise shifting cultivation. Java is, of course, an exception by virtue of her highly fertile, volcanic soil, already supporting a population rising to 70 million.

Equatorial soil fertility is rather low because much of it is laterite, a poor reddish soil, leached of its quality by the regular and heavy rainfall, but with so many agrarian developments it should not be long before much of this land could be cleared and maintained under crops. In fact, it should be capable of up to three crops a year, but tropical agriculture and farming faces more difficulties than temperate agriculture. The main difficulties are:

The rapid growth of vegetation. This helps crops, but

weeds also grow so rapidly that a farmer has a lot of trouble keeping them down, especially if he uses only primitive tools.

Diseases and insects attack plants more frequently and more virulently than in temperate lands.

Crops are much more difficult to preserve. They do not keep well in the damp heat and nobody has yet evolved really efficient storehouses proof against animals, insects and climate.

Despite the work being done on tropical soils the fact remains that we still know very little about the scope of tropical soils, partly because the nutrients of a tropical forest are found in living plants and not in the soil, because fungi and bacteria attack all plant waste and in practically no time trees and plants imbibe this waste. When somebody clears the land and begins cultivation the soil is without a protective cover and without a system of roots to take in the nutrients. Then, heavy rains again quickly leach the nutrients.

Dr. Mary McNeil has pointed out* that the ambitious plans to increase food production in the tropics to meet the pressure of the rapid rise of population have given too little consideration to the laterization problem . . . Laterization destroyed the Amazon Basin project in less than five years because the cleared fields became virtually pavements of rock.

Lack of good roads—they are non-existent in many areas —makes transport and sale of produce difficult. Roads that do exist are usually feet deep in mud and impassable during the rainy season. This applies to regions other than tropical areas—vast areas of Russia, for instance—but the tropics suffer more.

Stock are prey to insect attack and to climatic diseases. Animals still cannot be reared in parts of Africa.

Several native peoples living in tropical areas have

* *Scientific American*, November 1964.

reached only a relatively low intellectual standard, while others have long since had any will to work sapped by the exhausting conditions. Widespread tropical diseases further lower their efficiency.

Despite all these problems F.A.O. experts estimate that if only 20 per cent of the unused tropical soils could be cultivated, another $2\frac{1}{2}$ million hectares* would be added to the world's arable surface.

Some major scheme would be necessary to do this. It would cost a lot in effort and organization as well as money. It could only be a long-term plan and could not pay worthwhile dividends for several decades, but this is no excuse for not beginning it at all. It could make all the difference when the food and population problem reaches desperate proportions later in the century.

At the moment the value of tropical trade is not nearly so great as is generally believed. Certain articles of food such as tea, coffee, cocoa, sugar and rice play a reasonably large part, but none compare in value or bulk with trade in wheat and meat produced in the temperate zone. Of the tropical raw materials, rubber and the various types of hemp are the leading items, but trade in them does not approach in value the trade in wool, flax and wood pulp of the temperate zone. Fruit, spices and oil seeds make up most of the balance of trade from tropical regions. Meat, wool, wheat and dairy produce of the temperate zone are, after oil, Britain's leading imports by value. Sugar, tobacco, rubber and tea are the leading imports from tropical countries, but they rank only tenth to thirteenth on the list, and the value of each of these tropical products is only about a quarter of that of meat.

If the potential of some countries is over-estimated, that of other regions is not adequately assessed. The savannah areas of Australia, Africa, Uruguay and southern Brazil have enormous potential. These vast lands, used almost entirely

* One hectare equals approximately $2\frac{1}{2}$ acres.

for cattle grazing, could be farmed much more productively and effectively, though a lot of research and capital investment would be necessary. Australia has the greatest scope. It is reckoned that a further 160 million acres of land await development when they have been reinforced with trace elements and the soil quality has been increased by planting leguminous pastures. At present Australia produces a large amount of food on only 40 million acres.

Rain is generally restricted to summer, after which a long dry season sets in, but when water can be applied during this season—perhaps by pipeline from New Guinea—large parts of the country could be agriculturally exploited, without stealing too much land from the cattle stations. Fertilizers will probably be necessary.

Africa could produce more food than it does, though accurate assessment is impossible. Gradual, steady changes are preferable to big, ambitious attempts; the failure of the much-publicized ground-nut scheme in Kenya proves this. Foreign experts, much money, equipment and fertilizers are all necessary if real progress is to be made. Africa is wide open for foreign help—and will long remain so. Incidentally, it is ridiculous to charge an African country with leanings towards Communism merely because it happens to accept help from Russia or China. A backward nation will take help from anyone, for the main thing is survival.

Economic forces play a radical role in food changes, even in already prosperous countries, where the displacement, in part, of butter by margarine illustrates the principle. Entrenched traditional diets can be drastically influenced. In the Far East after 1945 rice was scarce and the price climbed prohibitively, so in Ceylon, India, the Philippines and Japan people began to use wheat and maize. In Ceylon rice is now plentiful but the taste for wheat and maize has persisted and in Japan it has increased. This dietary adaptability is more important than it might appear, for it provides the object lesson that if vegetables, fruit, milk and milk products, among others, could be made available at a lower cost, then they would be used even in areas where they have been unknown as part of diet. Bombay, for instance, has large-scale consumption of dried skim milk which is sold at low prices.

Despite the desperate need for action, the key to all successful development in the poorer countries is research about conditions of those countries. Skills and techniques acquired concerning one country will rarely transplant to others, even though basic ideas might well be adopted or adapted. At the World Food Congress in Washington in 1963 American delegates repeatedly stated that if only backward peoples were simply to work hard and copy U.S. techniques, they would be well fed in practically no time. This is not true. The U.S. has wasted billions of dollars on schemes fine in themselves but unrelated to the problems of particular countries.

Often there is a sound reason why undeveloped land is undeveloped. At one time U.S. cattle experts planned to develop more than 100,000 areas of Nicaragua into beef country. They had 'researched' the area, found it lush with grass and firm and flat, with well-spaced natural small lakes for watering, and voted it ideal. But the scheme fell flat, for the experts had seen the region during the one month of the year when conditions were perfect. After the heavy rains the whole place was a swamp; when it ceased and the ground dried it was bone hard, completely dry and with no grass at all. Impatience to do something must not override the necessity for research.

A crop or strain of a crop that will prosper in one area will not necessarily prosper in another. In another scheme that failed, blight-resistant potatoes from the eastern United States would not grow at all in Mexico, and only after a full 10 years' research was a suitable strain developed.

A less familiar aspect of crop protection and development is adaptation to wind and drought. Near harvest time many farmers in Europe find that wind has beaten flat much of a crop. The crop is then difficult to harvest and the farmer suffers financial loss. New plants can be dwarfed, without decreasing the yield, by feeding them with growth-regulating chemicals. Thus wind damage is reduced. Wind causes distinct changes in a plant's development and can especially upset the water balance. Intensive work is in progress to pre-adapt plants to wind and drought by treating them with chemicals known as anti-gibberellins. The commercial and human importance of anti-gibberellins will be vastly important, for many crops will be able to grow in areas of wind or drought not now used for agriculture. This is a fairly long-range project, but its potentialities are immense once laboratory theory is transferred to the field.

Sadly, a disaster is sometimes necessary to waken people to the need for progress. After the drought of 1960–1, followed by equally calamitous floods, the Masai tribes of Kenya lost 450,000 cattle. After decades of opposition to any change, these nomadic people saw that they must have an alternative to cattle. More and more of the 80,000 Masai people have co-operated in government-sponsored development projects and are now prosperous ranchers. They are still largely dependent on cattle, but grazing is now controlled, and is used and rested methodically.

It is a mistake to think that farmers in undeveloped countries are the only ones who are conservative and opposed to progress. They have been equally conservative in France, for instance. In the Midi, or that part of it west of the Rhône and bordering the Cevennes, farmers had for centuries been beset by drought during the summer months—drought relieved only by occasional devastating Rhône floods. The grape was the one crop which would grow here, but vines were stunted and poor, providing a low quality wine. The whole area was barren and desolate and in summer the ground was cracked like the mud pans of parts of India.

During the war of 1939–45 a farsighted farmer from

77

Northern France, Philippe Lamour, arrived in the region. He had ambitious plans to tap the Rhône with a long canal which would snake across the Midi, but to his dismay and surprise he found the farmers resistant and actively hostile. Walls were daubed with 'Death to Lamour', 'No canal in the Midi', 'Get out strangers' and other more abusive slogans. By sheer force of personality Lamour won popularity among the farmers, but he made no progress until he realized that example was necessary. He planted crops the way he wanted others to do and with great expense brought water to them. When they grew he invited farmers to see his crops—high, strong vines, strawberries—strawberries in the Midi!—vegetables, fruit. Example worked. The farmers accepted Lamour's plan, though a lesser man would have been discouraged by the many petty arguments that cropped up from time to time. Now 650,000 acres of the Midi are irrigated and prosperous, selling early fruit and vegetables in Paris and London among other places.

This rural prosperity proved the point, mentioned elsewhere in this book, that sound, healthy farming economy stimulates sound economy in other ways. When I saw the Midi coastline in 1957 it was lonely and deserted; in 1965 it was a popular tourist resort with miles of luxury hotels. These coastal settlements and cities like Arles and Nîmes provide a market not only for local agricultural produce, but for the beef cattle of the Camargue, a sub-region of the Midi. The case history of the Midi typifies the patience and persistence needed when trying to educate conservative people—and it is a universal axiom that most farmers are conservative.

6 TRADE AND AID

Professor J. E. Meade believes that the economic growth of underdeveloped countries has four main divisions. They are: investment in human resources, including technical assistance; aid in the form of capital loans or gifts; trade and, in particular, the purchase of the products of the underdeveloped countries by the developed countries; population control.

I doubt if he has listed them in what he might regard as their order of importance, for in fact the four divisions need equal attention and effort. Let it be said at once that a great many developments and projects exist and that a lot of money is given or lent to certain countries, but even in total they are akin in effect to a lone man bailing out a boat without any hope of stopping the leak. For instance, the Aswan High Dam will, by 1972, add 2 million acres of food-growing land to Egypt's agricultural area. By the same year the population will have increased by 13 million since the project started. Nobody will be any better off. It is literally true to say that nobody will gain a single extra grain of rice.

This is partly because no *single* line of attack on the problem of hunger has much chance of success. To put it bluntly, population must be curbed while food production increases. Also, many people lose sight of the distant goal of all development—a higher standard of living for ordinary people.

There is much specious talk about distribution of the surpluses which exist in some areas. It is true that there is enough grain and farm surpluses in the silos, warehouses, granaries and Liberty ship hulks in North America to give the 480 million people of India a year's supply of calories. In the United States alone 9,000 million dollars worth of grain is in store—at a storage cost of a million dollars a day. These vast reserves could provide every person in the whole of Asia with 200 calories a day for three years. This might give the impression that the U.S. is niggardly, but she has been quite generous with food, using it as currency and making it available 'on loan' to poor countries.* The government concerned, selling the wheat, can use the money to finance food and fertilizer projects. In any case, the surpluses are mainly cereals, when foods rich in protein are needed. The United States has distributed much dried milk, but there is a concealed drawback to this: it creates a demand for milk and milk products which cannot be satisfied by local sources.

Economic chaos could result if all surpluses were made a present of to needy countries. For instance, if the U.S. dumped her farm surpluses on the world market a balance of payments crisis would occur, a recession might follow and the needy countries would suffer more than they would be helped. Surpluses are minute in proportion to the need and, some experts feel that if they were introduced at low

* Apart from other aid, food bounty has flowed from the United States at the rate of three 10,000-ton shiploads per day since 1954.

cost into the underdeveloped countries, they might hit the development of food production in those countries.

Export surpluses of temperate zone food—and these are likely to increase—could best be handled by some sort of international fund. This fund, with the developed countries as contributors, would buy surplus food on the world market and distribute it to the hungry countries. Contributions to the fund would be estimated according to the general wealth of the country or in relation to its agricultural production.

Surpluses are increasing not only in the United States but in the European Economic Community as well, and nothing can stop them. Food output *per capita* in recent years in Western Europe has been growing at about twice the rate of growth of population. These surpluses are becoming a great problem to the European Common Market. Europe's agricultural-worker population is being reduced at an estimated $2\frac{1}{2}$ per cent annually, but the rise in agricultural productivity more than offsets this reduction. This happened in the United States in the 1940s and 1950s.

Encouraging increases are noticeable in other areas. In Eastern Europe and in the U.S.S.R. food production per head has risen 40 per cent since 1939, compared with the 15 per cent increase in Western Europe and North America. Even in the Near East food output has gone up 10 per cent. But these increases are marred by the situation in Latin America, Africa and the Far East, where production is less than in 1939.

The late Sir William Slater, when chairman of the U.K. Freedom from Hunger Projects Group, soberly warned* that 'Any source of cheaply available surplus (of food) is rapidly disappearing and we have to realize that all the efforts so far made have failed to provide the food needed to keep pace with the growing population . . . the food available *per capita* today is less than it was before 1939.'

* In an address, Hunger in an Angry World, Oxford, 1968.

In Western Europe dietary standards have been rising steadily, particularly with an increasing consumption of meat, poultry, butter and cheese. For instance, the average Frenchman now eats 18 kilograms more meat than he did in 1948 and 33 per cent more dairy products. At the same time consumption of cereals and starchy roots has declined, noticeably in Holland where average *per capita* consumption of roots is 85 kilograms lower than in 1948 and cereals 16 kilograms less.

Everybody is familiar with the much-publicized standard of living in the United States, but relatively few people realize that American prosperity, with all its current food surpluses and general creature comforts, cannot last more than another 10 years if the present rate of population growth continues. Taxes must rise very steeply to cope with public services; 30 billion dollars will be necessary for schools alone. More than this, as the United States grows she will want more and more of the world's resources; she already uses 52 per cent of all material resources, despite her 6.6 per cent of the world's population. But if the backward nations become industrialized—as they are trying to do—they will need to keep more of their raw materials.

No developed country lacks a healthy and large amount of industry. Australia, New Zealand and Denmark are labelled 'agricultural' countries, but they have many manufacturing industries and employ considerably less than half their labour forces in agriculture.

The lesson has obviously not been lost on India and Pakistan, on some East African countries and on Malaysia. Sooner or later all the countries whose economy now depends on exporting raw materials must reach a certain standard of industrialization if only to increase the standard of living of their own peoples. But while this is slowly happening, there is serious danger that the developed countries will waste their capital in aid and that the underdeveloped countries will feel a sense of stupendous disappointment unless population growth (discussed in another chapter) is ultimately controlled. In A.D. 2070 the world population will be eight times as large as it is now. This will mean ultimate misery and starvation for much of mankind, for no amount of economic effort can keep up with such an increase.

The problem of economy chasing population is not confined to countries such as India and China. In some underdeveloped countries the population is increasing by 3 per cent a year. This may not in itself seem very much, but to prevent decline in such a country's standard of living total output must rise by 3 per cent a year. On the assumption that £3 worth of capital equipment is needed to produce each £1 worth of output—and this is a fair basis—then the community must save 9 per cent of its real output and devote it to capital investment to increase future output merely to stop a fall in output per head. It is extremely difficult for a poor country to save 3 per cent, let alone 9 per cent of its national income.

The agricultural growth rate cannot even reach 3 per cent. With some exceptions, during the last decade the agricultural growth rate has averaged just over 2 per cent. The exceptions have been outstanding: Israel has averaged a 60 per cent increase in agricultural production and Mexico has more than doubled her output.

It is all so easy to say, but developing countries need to be more far-sighted, more economical, less concerned with immediate material benefits. Short-term high investment projects should defer to investment in education and other means of developing human resources and forming human capital. Meanwhile, various countries and agencies are contributing monetary capital. The amount of assistance being given to underdeveloped countries is variously estimated at between 5,000 million and 8,000 million dollars. The wide gap is probably due to differences in the items covered by various reports.

Regrettably, if you do a man a big enough favour he will

never forgive you. The same cynically true principle applies to nations, as can be clearly seen from the almost universal resentment of the United States. United States food surpluses, freely and usually unconditionally given, together with her massive financial aid, keeps many people alive—three million in Algeria alone—yet the same people, with others, merely vilify her. Americans have been hurt and disillusioned by the criticism, jealousy and spite that their open-handedness has caused. Their main fault has been their own naïveté and lack of caution, for sometimes a massive injection of aid money caused acute inflation, while at other times their money has given a crutch to governments which should have been allowed to fall.

The United States, in her political innocence—she is, after all, a relative newcomer to international politics and intrigues—often does not realize how complex a problem can be. She insists on a rigid policy and by her very attitude—regrettably ostentatious and patronizing—she irritates the countries and peoples she is trying to help. Not that veteran diplomatists such as the British and French are free of clumsiness and ineptitude: both still tend to act the colonial master. The Communist countries are newcomers to the game, and often clumsy, but Russia particularly is in a strong position for practising 'aidmanship' because many of the Asiatic countries are underdeveloped and Russia is herself an Asiatic power. 'We look after our own', she can say—and does say. The extraordinary paradox is that Russia herself is, in many ways, an underdeveloped country, especially judged by average annual income.

Charity is not enough. Many a man, knowing that he can depend on somebody else for a pound or a pudding, will not help himself. Simply giving a poor country food or money puts temptation in its way—the temptation to be idle. The best way to help a man and a country is to help it to help itself.

Also, where strings are attached to food or money grants

difficulties usually follow. This is why they are much better channelled through an international organization rather than offered and accepted directly from a wealthy country. Then the accusations of bribery, economic intimidation and economic imperialism cannot arise. Paul Hoffman has revealed that, 'representatives of countries receiving assistance repeatedly declare their preference for help through the United Nations, for one reason or other. From this source it is much more acceptable politically.'

Some governments cannot be trusted with aid money unless it is thoroughly protected; otherwise the money will be spent on arms. Some new African countries spend as much as 25 per cent of their budget on arms and perhaps another 15 per cent on militant African nationalism, which, ridiculously, is dedicated to apparently ceaseless enmity towards the West—the hand that so often feeds it.

Too much money is being spent on secondary and tertiary projects—beautiful roads, expensive buildings, even on observatories. West Germany has financed three such observatories in Chile. They hardly help the poverty-stricken masses of the country to eat more and better food. This is not true assistance.

Visitors are apt to get a very false impression from the façade presented by some countries. Rio de Janiero, Caracas, Lima, Havana, among others, are show-pieces with a glossy front of prosperity and satisfaction. It is not surprising that a visitor making a quick trip gains the idea that all is well, when, in fact, the luxury hides dreadful poverty.

Some countries put all the aid into the shop front and none into the workroom behind it. The cities look impressive, but the country is as neglected and backward as ever. To achieve the appearance of success the leaders put all aid money into the showy externals. They build new roads and line them with great apartment buildings, when the money would be better spent on irrigation ditches and an agrarian college. Most Latin American countries are shop-window states simply because their political set-ups made them that way.

More than half the farmland in Latin America is owned by less than 1 per cent of the population. A full 85 per cent of peasants own no land at all, and they work for a pittance for some wealthy landowner. This is a major cause of hunger. Throughout vast areas of the world poor people are being mercilessly exploited without hope of redress, short of armed rebellion or murder of landowners. This happens often enough in places like Colombia to make one imagine that other profiteers would reform, but such a hope is vain. Sometimes the rapacious landowners nip incipient rebellion in the bud by shooting possible ringleaders. The hatred between the miserable 'have-nots' and the luxury-loving big men is intense and evil. In such an atmosphere production and enterprise are stifled. The position seems hopeless because the great landowners of these countries—Chile, Ecuador and Peru among them—have too much influence politically. Land management in Latin America is not merely inept but terrifying, as René Dumont has so graphically pointed out in his *Terres Vivantes*.

Tying loan money to definite, approved projects has its advantages, for money from public or international funds is always liable to be sidetracked. A recipient country so often uses such money to attack the effects of poverty and not its causes.

Still, restrictions can be too hard and fast. Most lending agencies insist that money must be bound to something 'which can be seen'. Agriculture cannot, under the tight terms of the definition, be seen, so 'agricultural loan' money finds its way to large-scale irrigation schemes and dams. The small-scale agricultural projects—agricultural in the real soil-sense of the word—do not, in the tidy minds of leaders, constitute 'projects'. But these are just the schemes which could increase output greatly, as I show elsewhere. Similarly, seeds and fertilizers should qualify for loans, but rarely do.

Yet what else are they but items of capital expenditure?

Injections of money are important, but the right men are necessary to make the money work and there must be a favourable social climate in which it *can* work. This poses the problem of whether economic investments should have priority over social investments. Economic investment increases wealth—or is intended to do so; social investment increases all-round better living—'culture' might be a better word. Should money be spent on a dam or irrigation project or on a hospital or school? Some writers claim emphatically that only a small part of aid or development money should go on social investment. But they are working from a false base. The most important part of a nation's capital is its national health, both mental and physical. A nation cannot grow unless it believes in growth and has confidence in its efforts. People healthy in body and mind are much more likely to give their country this confidence.

Thus, money spent on social investment pays dividends in economy. The effect is quite noticeable in areas where social investment has been heavy, but unfortunately it cannot be shown on a balance sheet. Hence, at a casual glance, it appears not to be specially important. Of course, there can be no hard-and-fast ratio between money for economic and for social investment; the particular situation will fix the ratio.

What everybody must realize is that it takes time to learn new skills, and to produce cheaply one must have produced for some time and on a sufficiently large scale.

Developing nations need aid so desperately that they can have few scruples about where they obtain it. Guinea, a member of the French Union and really part of the French Republic, became independent in 1958. A month later she was negotiating with Soviet Russia and East Germany, later she negotiated with Red China, the United States and West Germany. But there is such a thing as too much aid—and the countries at the receiving end are more aware of it than the donors. Too many people are proposing aid without any co-ordination. Also, because their own resources are limited too much money can cause aid-inflation, which is too much money chasing too few goods. The capacity of a country to absorb aid must be studied.

Some countries, such as Jordan and Laos, receive direct subsidies; most of the states of the French communities receive budgetary subsidies. In 1961 the American Government, for some political reason, withheld the monthly aid to Laos. The Americans then discovered that the monthly payments were, in fact, the entire budget. In any case aid should not simply be doled out like a ration, as is the case with much American money paid to underdeveloped nations. Money should be given and received positively, for no country can use foreign aid effectively unless it receives it with a conscious will to use it productively.

The multilateral method of giving aid is a good one for any prosperous nation seeking a reason to limit commitments, because clearly the taxpayer and his government would give less to the United Nations than he would to personal friends. The United Nations or the World Bank can speak more bluntly to the Moroccans or the Zambians than can the Americans or the British, whose frankness might be misunderstood or lead to political repercussions. The bilateral method is best when dealing with huge amounts and quantities and when sensitive national interests are involved. Britain and the British might well want to give money to the Indians or Pakistanis from a sense of moral duty and the historic ties of centuries, but they might not wish to see British money sent to some Latin American country, whose difficulties could well be largely self-inflicted, or to a country whose politics they despise.

Dr. Paul Ehrlich, Professor of Biology and Director of Graduate Study in Biological Sciences, Stanford University, has proposed that the U.S., the Soviet Union, Britain, Canada, Japan, Australia, the countries of Western Europe and other developed countries set up machinery for 'area rehabilitation'. This plan would involve simultaneous population control, agricultural development and, where warranted, industrialization of selected countries or sections of countries. The basic requirements of this program would be population control, and migration control to prevent swamping of aided areas by the less fortunate. The approach would be through education and propaganda, designed in essence to show that only by making progress towards population control and self-sufficiency can they avoid disaster.

Aid is very often resented, but money earned through the sale of products is appreciated. Trade is a better method than aid of helping the underdeveloped to develop, but only if the prosperous countries refrain from using their full bargaining power, and if they accept the changes in their own economies which follow growth of trade with the underdeveloped nations. A wealthy nation might have to be mature enough to help an undeveloped country build up industries competitive with her own. The impact of this could be lessened by retraining and moving labour, and by tax remissions and adaptation allowances for the firms which might be hit by tariff cuts.

Developed countries are already good customers of the underdeveloped ones. Japan buys 58 per cent of her foreign purchases from non-industrialized countries, Britain 51 per cent, the United States 49 per cent and France 43 per cent.

Tropical underdeveloped countries seem to be peculiarly vulnerable, but I doubt if they have the soft underbellies that some economists suggest. They may be right when they say that there is not a single tropical commodity which the wealthy temperate countries must have, but there are a great many commodities they would like to have. The wealthy countries which do not aid the poorer countries now might well find them sending their raw materials—timber, rubber and tea, for example—to the nations which are willing to help them. The others will be left out in the cold. This is one main reason why West Germany has been courting the underdeveloped countries. She has built sugar mills in Kenya, Tanzania and Uganda; hundreds of the new factories appearing in India each year are German-financed; even the great observtories in Chile are built with German money and equipment. The Germans, astute businessmen, are building up an economic empire by being generous to all the developing nations. The investment cannot fail to pay dividends, for as these countries' standards of living rise, so they will buy German manufactured goods. No industrial country can consider itself self-sufficient or be complacent, not even the United States. In 1953 the Paley Commission reported to Congress that by as early as 1975 the United States will be 50 per cent dependent on raw materials and other resources from the underdeveloped countries.

The Germans in their aid projects do see the real value of trade. It is very important because it is the only method which will give permanent external resources to developing countries. And it is mutually beneficial. For this reason the developed countries can give more help to the underdeveloped countries, with less damage to themselves, by their commercial policy than by merely giving away material aid.

A shopkeeper prefers to be operating in a prosperous town, even in competition, because the more prosperous his neighbours the more goods he can sell, often at a higher price. The same analogy applies to the developed countries and the underdeveloped. The richer a developed country is the more it will demand the products of underdeveloped countries, especially their raw materials. Hence successful domestic policies in a developed country promote prosperity in some underdeveloped country. The process must be watched: a country such as Britain could develop its economic expansion to the point where it might be importing so much that its balance of payments would be threatened.

Many underdeveloped countries, as they progress, must have export markets for their produce. This may be in the

form of markets for greater supplies of primary products
(tropical foodstuffs from Africa or tin and rubber from Malaysia), or for highly processed primary products (aluminium rather than bauxite, its raw material; refined copper
rather than crude copper), or for cheap-labour manufactures (such as textiles from Hong Kong or India). Many
countries cannot hope successfully to develop efficient economies on the basis of self-sufficient production. They need
enlarged export markets to buy products, when they learn
to produce cheaply on a large scale, and to finance a great
part of their expanded need for imported food, raw materials, capital goods and high-precision consumer goods.

The developed countries must lower their barriers against
imports from the underdeveloped countries. If anybody is
to use protection as a means of improving terms of trade,
it should be the poor, not the rich countries. The ideal—
which selfish, narrow interests probably makes impossible
—would be for the developed countries to amalgamate as a
huge free trade area, a 'free' market with no real obstacles
to whatever the underdeveloped countries want to export.
The scheme could succeed only if the United States, the
European Economic Community and the United Kingdom
agreed to co-operate.

The standard of living in underdeveloped countries could
be greatly helped by market expansion for their primary
products. Oil is an exceptional case, but it has shown dramatically how a country can benefit by increased demand
for a particular product. The economy of small, backward
states which strike oil is transformed practically overnight.
But while there is no barrier to oil trade, other raw materials
suffer from import barriers. For example, the United States
has barriers against zinc and lead in order to protect home
producers. These barriers seriously hamper some underdeveloped countries.

As a further example, imagine how badly hit some underdeveloped countries would be if Western nations banned

smoking or raised tobacco duty to even more prohibitive heights. Even is smoking is not banned it seems likely, following medical research in the U.S., Britain and France, that there will be intensive anti-smoking campaigns. The hard-hitting 'Smoking Kills' report by British doctors in January 1971 and its demand for government action is just one indication that smoking could decrease. Increased life expectancy in some countries will mean a lower standard of living in those countries for which tobacco is a staple export, as in Central and South America, Africa and parts of Asia.

The basic trade problem for the underdeveloped countries is this: will the highly developed countries provide them with large and expanding markets for their manufactures? India and Hong Kong, for example, produce vast amounts of textiles very cheaply and they depend on sales in Western countries for their profit margin. Barriers raised against these textiles prevent expansion in India and Hong Kong and keep people out of work—and therefore hungry. We talk so glibly of trade and industrial development that we tend to forget that the very food people put in their mouths depends on it. Trade and hunger are intimately connected. Again, it is probably best to appeal to the self-interest of the developed nations. By raising incomes and standards of living in the backward countries they are creating a vast new market for their goods. This market will open to the West at a speed consistent with the amount of help given to the backward countries.

Unfortunately, world economic development has largely become a weapon of cold-war propaganda. This is why administration and distribution of financial aid through the United Nations is preferable. It links the governments of the underdeveloped and of the developed countries in a world operation for world economic development. The cold war has an illogical effect on aid money. The United States' distribution of money, in 1957 for instance, was a case in point. She gave about half the money available to

three countries—South Korea, Formosa and South Vietnam. These countries then had a total population of about
40 million, but they received as much aid money as all the
other inhabitants of the non-Communist underdeveloped
countries, with a total population of 1,150 million. Politically this might make sense, but the countries who receive
relatively little of the American bounty often feel sour about
it. Too often aid money has an unpleasant taste of competition: 'We will give you a hundred million dollars if you
don't enter into any agreement with the other side.' In 1958
the U.S.S.R. and Eastern Germany retracted promises of
aid to Yugoslavia because Marshal Tito was unwilling to
rejoin the Eastern bloc.

David Lilienthal, an American who heads a private development company, has produced a practical six-point philosophy for tackling the food problem in the underdeveloped
countries. It is not a practical *plan* but a plan might well be
built on the philosophy, provided always that population is
controlled.

These are Lilienthal's points:

Treat feeding people for what it is: a business, not a
mystique, not primarily an opportunity for social reform
and uplift. People who raise and process and distribute
food are first and foremost just another kind of private
businessmen. You don't have to teach the tiller of the
soil about the profit system: he practically invented it.
Give him a chance for a profit and he will do most of the
rest.

Don't over-plan. Give the producer, whether he's an
independent farmer or a corporate farm manager, a chance
to exercise spontaneity.

Farming must, for the most part, be on a large scale.
Bigness is as important an essential for food-plenty as
it has been in the mass production of the mechanical and
electronic aids that men everywhere now demand.

Government must believe that it is in the public interest that farmers and food producers make money, even get rich, if they can. If they get too rich at the expense of others, tax them; but don't dry up the driving force that will produce food by too many government controls.

Food production must not be treated as a happy hunting ground to advance the professional prestige of scientists and economists. Food production is simply part of the *business of getting food to people*, changing (i.e. manufacturing) what is grown into other forms, and making *distribution* as much a respected skill as *developing* new strains of wheat.

The key to feeding the world is *management*. Treat land as an asset to be managed, as other physical assets are treated in industry. The methods of management, innovation, respect for arithmetic, and understanding of human nature that have grown up in industry must be applied to agriculture.

This philosophy has the faults of anything evolved by American Big Business. For instance, it does not take into account what is to be done with the millions of peasant farmers displaced by 'bigness' in farming. But it is realistic in its recognition of the profit motive and the need for expertise.

7 THE 'GREEN REVOLUTION'

The very phrase 'green revolution' implies hope but it might well have been mischievously evolved by those people who oppose population control on religious grounds or by those incurable optimists who consider that the situation is not as bad as it is said to be. The success of high yielding cereals in some countries has led to a belief that the world is in the midst of this 'green revolution', which will solve all the major problems of agricultural development in the poorer countries.

Certainly, the development of some cereals in some places has been impressive. In 1968, 1969 and 1970 the Philippines harvested record rice crops with about 15 per cent of the nation's rice fields planted with the 'miracle' rice, IR-8 and IR-5, developed at the International Rice Research Institute at Los Banos with the help of the Rockefeller and Ford Foundations. The yield has been 15 times higher than that of standard strains.

Some African countries—Cameroons, Gabon, Gambia, Malawi, Niger and Senegal—have introduced from China the Taiwan Native 1 rice species and have more than doubled production obtained from traditional rice strains. New wheat strains have also produced high yields, notably in India and Pakistan. But the biggest increases will come, as always, in the developed countries. F.A.O.'s agricultural predictions for the next 30 years in the U.S. are that wheat will jump to 300 bushels an acre compared with the 30 of 1970, that corn will reach 500 bushels an acre, from the 75 of 1970. These predictions disturb the American Government considerably for, while the U.S. will need extra food for its growing population, it already has an embarrassing surplus.

The situation of the Green Revolution is much more complex. The new seeds by themselves provide only *potential* progress. They will give full yields only if planted with the right kinds and qualities of fertilizers in the right amounts and protected by the correct amounts and types of insecticide. They need great extension of irrigation, better tools, more training for the peasant farmer, better storage, distribution, marketing and credit facilities. The number of food crops in which high yielding varieties have so far been successfully grown is still small. More research is needed to increase and improve them and to adapt those already developed to widely differing soils and climates.

The new varieties at present affect less than 6 per cent of the cereal area in the developing countries. In 1968–9 they probably contributed less than 10 per cent of additional cereal production in those countries. In the future, they could be grown in up to one third of the total world cereal area and contribute up to 50 per cent of the total cereal output, provided there is considerable capital investment in irrigation, drainage, flood control, insecticide and fertilizers.

Comparatively little attention has been paid to improving varieties of winter and hard or 'durum' wheats, barley, sorghum and millet and rice suitable for areas with poor irrigation facilities or subject to flooding. This means that large areas have no share in the 'green revolution'. In Asia, only 20 per cent of the rice is grown under controlled irrigation and in the Near East under one third of the wheat and barley. Almost all the 30 million hectares of sorghum and millet in Africa and 26 million hectares of maize in Latin America is not irrigated.

The pattern of land allocation to cereals in some countries is distorted by high prices for certain products. This applies especially to the prices for wheat as compared with those for coarse grains. In these countries a major research effort is needed to improve cereal breeding and agronomy and to determine economic factors in the use of fertilizers and other 'inputs'. The United Nations Food and Agriculture Organization regards this as a 'First Generation' problem of crucial importance which demands both technical and financial support from the developed countries.

Wherever the 'green revolution' is apparently succeeding, it brings with it a host of complex and interlocking problems, particularly in storage, transport and drying. As more countries approach self-sufficiency and as weather sometimes leads to sudden surpluses, these difficulties are likely to become more severe. There must be national and international action to even out unpredictable production fluctuations, to prevent waste and to stabilize prices. A major priority is to improve the storage-transport-marketing chain and to provide cheap and effective storage at village level. Britain's Tropical Stored Products Centre is already doing pioneer work. The U.K. Freedom from Hunger Campaign Committee has adopted post-harvest food losses as one of its major targets for action and is financing a number of storage protection projects in Kenya, Ethiopia and Zambia.

The 'miracle' rice and wheat strains are not enough by themselves to ensure the successful fruition of the green revolution. To begin with, there must be a will for improvement within the developing nations. The people of the food-deficient nations must be sure that it pays to invest in new seeds, fertilizer, pesticides, and farm machinery. And their governments, savings institutions and businessmen must provide the credit, marketing, and other services and facilities to make the whole system of modern agriculture run.

The governments of the developing nations, their private institutions and their farmers cannot sustain this green revolution without outside support. They lack the skills to do the adaptive research, the foreign exchange to import fertilizer, the capital to build fertilizer plans, and the facilities and technicians needed to train the populace in modern agricultural techniques.

The kind of support and advice can come only from the developed nations directly or through international agencies.

Where is the farmer—and especially the small farmer—to find the money to buy himself into the 'green revolution'? How is he to pay for the extra fertilizers and insecticides, the additional drainage and the partial mechanization which is sometimes necessary to get the best results? Adequate bank, co-operative or government credit is not always easy to achieve. The recurrent costs to farmers, and foreign exchange demands upon national budgets are still holding back a really large-scale development of the high yielding varieties in many of the poorer countries. So far, member countries of F.A.O. have not regarded with favour proposals for a pool of 'inputs' as part of aid, organized on the lines of the World Food Program. The Second World Food Congress at The Hague in June, 1970, recommended governments to have another look at these proposals.

While the small farmer in the developing countries stands in the greatest need of the potential benefits of the high yielding varieties, it is the large farmer who has the resources with which to reap the maximum advantage. In India and Pakistan, in Mexico and in Turkey, the main benefits have gone to the medium and larger farmer in areas of high potential. These farmers are better equipped to absorb the price reductions needed to allow economic concentrate feeding of livestock. These reductions are reflected in wheat and rice prices. They have been ploughing back profits in a degree of mechanization which has as its object not only higher productivity but also a displacement of labour even in areas where there is already a labour surplus. Properly organized, the new cereal technology can increase labour requirements but *laissez faire* mechanization can have the reverse effect.

This is all the more serious because many developing countries face mounting rural unemployment and a flight to the towns where few jobs are available.

There are often seasonal work bottlenecks in agriculture which can be broken by part mechanization leading to a further productive use of labour. There is no solid evidence that full-scale mechanization leads to increased output although it does give individual farmers greatly increased profits. It does not help the smaller farmer who lacks adequate work power at peak times and suffers from 'diseconomies of scale' because he has to maintain draught animals throughout the year.

It has been suggested that the Intermediate Technology Organization might develop a scheme for part mechanization of key operations on small farms combined with work patterns which demand the maximum use of human labour for other operations. Unless the smaller farmers can be helped in this way and given the supporting package of credit, advisory and marketing institutions, the 'green revolution' will either be taken over almost entirely by large-scale enterprises, thus forcing the small man on to the already swollen labour pool, or it will run out of steam.

Improving the conditions of the small farmer may lead to some slowing down in the growth of food supplies as well as to higher government expenditure on agriculture.

But in the long run, the progress of the peasant farmer is the key to agricultural advance in the developing countries. There is little that aid agencies can do to prevent large private farmers adopting any policies they wish. But by giving support to the right kinds of projects and institutions, such as the produce marketing boards in East African countries and the Pueblo scheme in Mexico, they can do a great deal to help governments to develop ways of raising production, income and employment on small farms. They can also sponsor agro-industries together with linked farm production programs which would lead to a further improvement of rural living standards.

The major gap in calorie supplies lies mainly in Asia and the Near East where the potential for the use of high-yielding varieties is fairly high and success in their wider adoption in these areas could plug this gap for the next 15 years. Longer-term research would help to boost this impetus over a longer period. This would not solve the problem of improving protein quality, especially among farmers with low incomes who can rarely afford meat. This underlines the importance of the work on high protein food additives, protein cereals with a higher amino acid content and rice with a higher total protein composition now being carried out in many countries.

Meat is still the prime source of protein. But in the immediate future, plans for expanded meat production such as expanded cattle-ranching and game-cropping in Africa are unlikely to produce the vast amounts of increased animal protein likely to be in demand. A faster growth of pig and poultry production is one practicable way of helping to close the protein gap. In addition to the production of enriched high protein cereals, another way is to improve yields of food legumes such as pulses, groundnuts and soya and, where possible, to increase the area in which they are grown. At present these crops are being pushed out of the better areas by the more profitable high-yielding cereals and output in some countries is declining. International, widely spread research is vital in genetic engineering, disease control and improved farm practices.

Outside the 'green revolution', agriculture in the developing countries faces an equally difficult problem—what to do with the 'bad lands'—the areas where the crop potential is so low that it is not considered worth while to sow the new seeds. Two measures would help—the encouragement of mixed farming together with a closer integration between livestock and crops and an increase in legume production. The higher unit price of many legume crops would enable them to compete well with cereals in places where high-yielding varieties cannot be grown. In time, as cereal agronomy in higher areas improves, and high-yielding varieties of high protein crops are developed, a further change of land allocation between cereals and other crops should be possible.

The improvement of standards of living in the 'bad lands' is more important than the problems of individual crops. It demands an extremely broad approach in which success is only probable through a major international scientific and socio-economic programme covering many branches of knowledge. This is unlikely to achieve the spectacular results of the high-yielding varieties but it is equally essential if an unsupervised 'green revolution' is not to lead to widening gaps between rich and poor areas and the disintegration of the 'bad lands' into semi-deserts.

The 'green revolution' without direction spells anarchy. Properly controlled within a comprehensive agricultural policy, it can contribute enormously to the advancement of the farmer during the Second Development Decade.

Dr. Addeke Boerma, Director-General of F.A.O., told the Second World Food Congress at The Hague in June 1970, 'The green revolution is in itself not enough. Its benefits must reach all classes of society.'

8 EDUCATION—THE ROOT OF THE PROBLEM

Somebody has said—I think it was H. G. Wells—that civilization is a race between education and disaster. Education, despite desperate efforts to flog it along, is not winning the race. Basically, there are two reasons for this. The supply of teachers cannot keep pace with the increase in the number of people to be educated, and many authorities have not realized that education has a direct and profound influence on food production.

In November 1959 Sir Julian Huxley said, 'Feeding most people is determined by old customs. Millions of ignorant or prejudiced people have to be persuaded to alter their habits and bring them into line with modern knowledge'.

The education of people has two aspects: one short-term, the other long-term. The short-term policy is to attempt a general mass education about major facts of food and agriculture—and, of course, birth control. The long-term plan involves the more or less conventional education of child-

102

ren. Both need to be forcefully pushed along.

Morocco has already shown that bold, vigorous action can bring about an almost immediate re-education of people in their attitude to food. In August 1959 the government sent loudspeaker vans into the suburbs of Rabat and Casablanca to urge people to eat fish. One slogan was: You get as much nourishment from one and a half pounds of fish as you could from one pound of meat for only a quarter of the cost.

By publicizing and pushing fish in the press and through radio and the cinemas, the government caused a remarkable change in the public attitude even in the inland regions. Queues of more than 2,000 people formed to buy fish at the quays. Now Morocco has about 2,400 fishing craft and fish consumption is gratifying, but still the catch is only a portion of what it could be.

The difficulties of teaching people to eat fish can hardly be imagined, even in countries where fish forms a natural part of diet. In Senegal a spirited attempt was made to sell various fish foods to villagers living no more than five miles from the sea. The effort failed, partly because women thought that eating fish would make them sterile.

An analysis of the problem of world education is frightening and discouraging; it is a case of lighting a small candle rather than railing at the darkness. Perhaps the magnitude of the problem is itself good enough reason for not being discouraged by it, but it is just as well to realize its depth.

It is so easy to say glibly that as today's children grow up conditions must improve, to say that as education spreads so will better living conditions. This is theory. The fact is that population growth outstrips inroads into illiteracy and that at least 50 per cent of the world's children have no chance of receiving any education. The following illiteracy percentages give some idea of the magnitude of the problem: India 83.4; Africa 80; Brazil 51; Peru 52.

U.N.E.S.C.O. estimates that about 45 per cent of all

people over 15 years of age cannot read or write. Many of them are without the basic formula for mere survival, in the form of simple facts about agriculture and health. How can a farmer who is unable to read, possibly find out how to improve his lot? One development after another, one agricultural or technological break-through following hard on its predecessor help the already successful farmer of the prosperous countries. Farmers of the backward countries never hear of these developments and so still lean heavily on superstition and outdated methods. In Sicily, where profound rural poverty and hunger goes hand in hand with city wealth, many farmers will not use manure because they regard it as unclean. In India dung is used almost exclusively as fuel.

Education must be concerned with such simple practical matters as teaching underprivileged farmers to plough and plant on the contour, that is, around a slope and not up and down it. Up-and-down planting causes erosion and loss of water, but it can still be seen in many parts of the world. British farmers have learned about contour farming, but some still use tracks and roads that run straight up a slope, thus inviting these lines to become gullies in due course.

Traditional attitudes are a stumbling block. In parts of India a man is revered if he manages to father many sons. In Latin America men feel that by producing large numbers of children they are proving their masculinity; they are not interested in how their wives feel about it or how the children are to be fed.

The contrast between educated and unskilled farming is sometimes seen in the same area. Near Cholburi, Thailand, is a large manioc plantation employing 375 workers and providing factory work for another 200. The factory, which turns the manioc roots into tapioca, is Thailand's largest. Much manioc is supplied by small farmers in the large district around Cholburi, but these small farmers simply do not understand that they must replenish the soil. Despite intensive efforts by the plantation manager, Phra Chuang-kashetra, in five years their soil is worn out and the farmers must sell at a loss and move away. The plantation does not use commercial fertilizers but cow dung and plant waste; both are available for the small farmers, but Phra Chuang-kashetra has met only frustration and exasperation in his self-imposed attempts to enlighten them.

The peasant farmer's reluctance to try something new is human and understandable. He knows too well that failure means disaster and it is difficult to convince him that the risk of failure is remote. He has no capital to withstand a failure. The penalty is starvation for him and his family.

In the Philippines peasant farmers rely on the sacrifice of pigs and chickens to bring fertility and high yield to their rice crops. Probably they would not use fertilizers even if given them.

Many primitive and semi-primitive people think only of filling their stomachs—a natural and human enough desire considering their abject circumstances. Yet very often a small amount of food with high nutritional value in place of part of the habitual bulk would cost no more. Educational schemes are apt to run into difficulties unless the educators take into account the significance of food for many people.

Familiar food gives a sense of security; in fact, it is the only security many people and some races possess. During the 1845-6 potato famine in Ireland, America sent great quantities of maize to help the Irish, but they rejected it wholesale. So acute was the dislike for this new food—new to the Irish—that some people starved rather than eat it. Starving people in parts of Asia have similarly rejected wheat and millet, for backward people need a major psychological readjustment to change from a lifetime of rice-eating. In 1945 pea-soup powder was sent to Italy to feed the people left hungry because of the war, but the Italians ate it with extreme reluctance.

Dietary limitations based on religion have a profound influence on food-health. Mohammedans may not eat pork, most Hindus will not eat beef and other Hindus will not eat any animal food except milk because their faith prohibits the taking of life. The Jewish religion bans pork, shellfish and other foods. Any change in religious dietary habits can occur only over a very long period, as will habits based on superstition. In some countries animal flesh is repugnant because animals are regarded as 'friends of man'. This applies especially to horses and dogs, both used as food in some countries, just as locusts, snails, mice, frogs, snakes, grubs are subject to taste and distaste. Even milk is a 'disputed' food. In many countries it is regarded as essential to health and delicious as well, but to some people it is disgusting. Senegalese women believe it will make them barren. The great differences in attitudes to food must be considered in food education programmes, but the common-sense world aim should be to bring about a more equitable distribution of food.

Language is another factor working against education. India for instance, has 14 major languages. Hindi, spoken widely in north-central India, is the official language, but more than half the population will have to learn it from the beginning, adding to the tremendous problem of education. Many Indians never will learn it and some states—those who speak the Dravidian language—have even demanded secession from the Indian union. The same problem bedevils education in China and parts of Africa.

Malaise, yet another hurdle, can reach extreme proportions. Several field workers have reported cases of illiterate peasant farmers induced to grow heavy-yielding maize or other crops. Having found that the crop yielded twice as much as before the farmers planted only half the area next season. The situation is tragic-comically frustrating, but not so illogical as it seems. If he has a surplus a farmer must have some way of selling it; also he must have something to spend his profit on. In numerous areas when both these have been provided many native farmers have willingly increased their production.

Probably the most sinister influence militating against education is the belief of some highly educated leaders of backward countries that education only makes people unsettled and that a country's best ends are served by keeping the common people ignorant. Some politicians genuinely believe this; others practise the precept for their own ends. The belief of all too many leaders seems to be that the masses, while certainly poor, are content enough; educate them and they are still poor but no longer happy. Unfortunately there is some truth in this.

Other administrators hold the callous, even inhumane, view that in areas where life expectancy is so short money spent on education is wasted. A minor Pakistani official in Karachi told me that until average life expectancy reached at least 40 money devoted to education is 'bad business'. However, the investment made by any country in its teachers and other professional men is paying off much more today than a few decades ago when they lived for only 20 or 21 years. In India, Pakistan and Latin America life expectancy for such people is now 32, and increasing.

Some governments and their officials regard education as a mere consumption or social expenditure, and extravagant and wasteful at that. They themselves must be educated to realize that the battle of food production and over-population can be won in the classroom.

This is proved by an F.A.O. and U.N.I.C.E.F. accomplishment in the Indian state of Orissa, where somebody had the simple but effective idea of teaching school children to care for food grown in school gardens. The basic idea was not only to produce food but to use the children as disciples to preach food appreciation to the more ignorant adults. Usually councils of elders provided the children with land, but at Ramchanda they were unco-operative, so the advice of the F.A.O. field adviser was sought. He suggested that the children build hanging gardens they did just this, using the traditional bullock wagon bamboo baskets, each about six feet long and two feet wide. They filled them with silt scraped from river valleys and cattle dung collected in the streets and supported them by crossed stilts, well clear of the ground and sometimes in layers. The monsoonal rains filtered through the soil and did not damage the gardens, as so frequently happens in parts of the Indian sub-continent.

U.N.I.C.E.F. gave the children seeds—beans, peas, tomatoes—and with each basket producing three crops a year each child in the scheme gets plenty of good quality food. The obvious lesson has to do with education but for the far-sighted there is another lesson: when land runs out or in areas where normal gardens are impracticable for one reason or another gardens can always be suspended or held up.

An investment is made with the expectation of getting a return. By creating trained young minds and creating sane attitudes the world will get a return, as in Orissa. As a simple example, if the children of Sicily were to be educated properly the ancient superstitious reluctance to use animal manure on farm fields would be eliminated and, of course, the fields would have a heavier yield. To the individual, schooling is a definite means of increasing his future earnings; the same principle applies, collectively, to the nation.

No country in Asia, Africa or Latin America could have too much education, although they could have the wrong kind of education, and no amount imaginable is too much to spend. The most urgent need of newly independent nations and of the older but equally backward ones is to build up a corps of educationists; without it they cannot hope to be modern, democratic or progressive. First priority should go to a high standard of education for a limited but large enough section of the population to supply the leadership in political, administrative and economic fields, and the personnel for essential services, industrial and agricultural development and scientific research.

One of the best immediate plans for more food is effective exploitation of lands already in use. The 'mechanics' of farming are simple enough, but millions of people do not understand them. Plants and crops take from the soil several chemicals vital for their growth—nitrates, potassium, phosphates, for example. These are to plants what calories, proteins and vitamins are to animals, including humans. Soil must have nutrition to compensate for the nutrients being taken from it. In the natural order plants die and fall and their content is returned to the earth, but in farming this sequence is interrupted when the crops are removed. When the same crop is grown in the same soil year after year the soil deteriorates. By growing different crops in rotation and by periodically returning the fields to grass the balance can be kept, particularly if beans, peas, clover, or lucerne are part of the rotation. These plants take nitrogen from the air and change it into nitrogen compounds; when ploughed under this nitrogen content supplements soil quality.

Farmers, such as those in Britain who have been practising rotation for many generations, become impatient with the millions of farmers who do not use it at all. The trouble is that many of them have never heard of it and would not understand it if they did. Also, a Pakistani who has been growing wheat or a Burmese who has been growing rice all his life and who must grow it to make his miserable income, cannot be expected suddenly to change his crop. This is where education must come into the food problem.

Unskilled agriculture does more harm than good. It was responsible, for example, for the 'dust bowls' in the United States and for erosion in hundreds of areas throughout the world. The dust bowls prove that to produce greater amounts of food *at whatever cost* is shortsighted. We would be damning our descendants and sentencing them to hunger.

109

Education must begin by wiping out or reducing illiteracy, but it cannot end there. Vocational education and training in agriculture and conservation, food production and marketing and distribution must also be provided. Raising levels of nutrition will depend partly on education of the consumer; people should make the right choice of food. It is frustrating that even when necessary foods are abundantly available millions do not follow a sound diet. Much malnutrition has been found even in the United States, Australia and Sweden. A person's diet may be lacking in vitamins, minerals or proteins. People must be educated as to what kinds of food are essential to health and how to produce or obtain the right foods or adequate substitutes.

The first world conference on Agricultural Education and Training was held in Copenhagen in September 1970 by three U.N. agencies—U.N.E.S.C.O., F.A.O. and I.L.O. It became clear during this conference that the safest prediction about the future of agricultural education is that it will become less agricultural, that more food will be grown by fewer people.

Here, we have the start of the process upon which the Industrial Revolution was based: higher farm productivity releasing a labour supply for cities where it is gobbled up by burgeoning mills. But the pattern of 19th century Europe cannot be repeated in the developing continents of the 20th century. There is already an exodus from farms to cities, but often into *favellas, bidonvilles,* shanty-towns and other new urban slums for the jobless. Nor is there so much to be recommended in megalopolis on the Western model.

Professor Sir Joseph Hutchinson of the School of Agriculture at Cambridge University told the conference that planners of agricultural education today must keep in mind, as their first priority, the possibility that many of their students will not stay on farms. This was not to say that they should move into urban areas in the way that the farming populations of the West moved under the compulsions of the Western Industrial Revolution. In India, it was apparent that the great majority of those now in the countryside would have to remain there. There was no other source of livelihood in the country besides farming so political pressure for subdivision of holdings in land was very great.

Sir Joseph believes that 'imaginative development of agricultural education to cover the needs . . . of rural living offers the best prospect of avoiding the misery and degradation that has accompanied urbanization on the Western pattern.'

He defines such development as the transformation of the agricultural education system into one of rural education at levels from the primary school to the university. As an example, he cited the introduction of 'locally-oriented biology' into a curriculum instead of mere school gardens. Economics and the other social sciences probably would follow, but with a rural slant.

It was the same specialist who has noted that it is only in agriculture that governments feel obliged to provide an advisory service. He sees no reason why such services should not go to the small businessman or craftsman. He suggests that the proliferation of small businesses be encouraged as a means of maintaining a reasonable dispersion of the population and facilitating the inevitable transfer of people out of agriculture.

Some governments are trying to provide greater incentives for remaining on the land. This can be done partly through economic development, through improving agriculture, medical care and housing. But in the long term it must come also through education. The academic routine must be modified to meet rural needs; it must be made more practical and vocational. Most African States have programmes for ruralizing aspects of their education, helped in many cases by U.N.E.S.C.O. or bilateral aid. But not always is it easy to see what precisely needs to be done and many African teachers are torn between their awareness of the need for

111

change and their reverence—sometimes excessive—for the European academic standards they have inherited.

The system needs to be thought out anew. One of the most inspired moves in this direction is a new pilot training college for rural primary teachers at Yaoundé, run by the Cameroon Government and staffed by U.N.E.S.C.O. with funds from U.N.I.C.E.F. and the U.N. Development Programme. It is the Ecole Normale d'Instituteurs à Vocation Rurale, known as E.N.I.R.

At E.N.I.R., a new rurally-oriented curriculum is being devised empirically, with the 70 young trainees (including some 15 girls) being used as guinea-pigs. The aim is to train a new type of teacher, one who can prepare both children and adults for a better integration into the social and economic life of their village and their country. It is an imaginative scheme, and the U.N.E.S.C.O. staff—Swiss, Belgian, Czech, French, Greek and others—have eagerly worked out a new primary syllabus, hoping that one day a national network of these teacher-animators will be able to improve rural life and to encourage peasants to build a better existence on the land.

The project ties in with another rural one near Yaoundé, led by an Israeli team who have helped to build a pilot village in bush country 25 miles from the city. With flair and energy these pioneers of the Negev bulldozed new farming land out of the thick bush, and built a village of neat white concrete bungalows for 50 families. By introducing farming and marketing methods unknown here before, they helped the village to increase their incomes up to 15-fold and some were able to buy luxuries undreamed-of, such as motorcycles and transistors.

People all over the world need a lot of instruction in the preparation of food so as to obtain the greatest nourishment from it and to avoid illness. For instance, in Thailand and elsewhere some people eat their meat and fish raw and consequently suffer from worm diseases. In Western coun-

112

tries housewives boil the goodness out of many vegetables, while in the East some of the methods of preparing rice remove practically all this cereal's nutritive value. Even in the so-called advanced countries people need to be educated to the possibilities of 'strange' food, as I have mentioned in the chapter on sea foods. Americans, for instance, eat only nine main species of fish and refuse to touch any of the other 24,991 types.

The agriculturally prosperous, developed and efficient nations of the world could well help the backward ones by 'importing' farmers from these places to show them how a modern high-yield farm works. This would be practical education and example and would achieve more than any volume of oral exhortation and paper education. People of the developed countries are apt to forget that most of their farmers were at one time very backward and have learned by example. This applies even to the Americans, reluctant though some of them are to admit it.

The first Anglo-Saxons to practise irrigation on the American continent were members of the Church of Jesus Christ of Latter-Day Saints—the Mormons. When the Mormons arrived in the arid Utah plain which was to be their home they had no experience of irrigation, but during their long trek from the fertile east they had noticed water conservation practices of some Indian tribes. They diverted a small mountain stream, flooded a few acres of barren-looking soil and grew potatoes. The Mormons were the first people in America to show the possibilities of large-scale irrigation in the American deserts, and that they succeeded because their religious disciplines made them uniquely co-operative only adds to their achievement.

The Mormons' leader, Brigham Young, insisted that no man should own more land than he could personally cultivate. Mechanization and modern techniques have increased the size of many Utah farms to more than 300 acres, but many farms of 10 and 20 acres are still intensively worked.

The chief products of these irrigated Utah farms are poultry and livestock, alfalfa, wheat, barley, potatoes, sugar beet, peas, peaches, tomatoes, oats, cherries, apples, apricots, onions, strawberries, pears and celery. Due to careful irrigation practices and intensive cultivation the yield on these farms is well above the national average, although the arable strip takes up only 5 per cent of the state.

Utah's farms are an object lesson for similar schemes in other desert areas. They have already done so in the United States, for the great Californian Valley irrigation schemes, among the world's most successful, were based on techniques evolved in Utah. No two areas have exactly the same problems, even when in the one country, but the achievements in one can often be applied to another, perhaps with modifications. This is why one of the greatest gifts the developed nations could bestow on the backward ones would be the opportunity for selected farmers to see for themselves how a modern farm operates. It is pointless to pour money into projects and schemes if the farmers living in them are not capable of taking full advantage of them.

Research is merely a form of education. There could be no better example of an investment paying high dividends than in the case of the United States research programme into hybrid corn. The country spent 131 million dollars on this programme, but in 1955 gained an additional income of 900 million dollars from corn. This represented a 700 per cent return on the investment. If this could occur in a country with an already enviably high agricultural standard, research could accomplish even more in backward areas, yet the governments of several countries allocate no funds at all to research, which they regard as a wasteful academic activity.

Nigerian, Ghanaian and Cingalese politicans have told me, in practically the same words, that research neither wins votes nor enhances their reputation. 'If research had obvious and immediate dividends everybody would vote funds for it,' one official told me. The F.A.O. and other United Nations bodies have been fighting a stand-off battle for years in an attempt to overcome this prejudice.

A 'knowledge' bank would be a useful adjunct to research, so that previous experience could be drawn upon and previous mistakes avoided. The F.A.O. has such a bank, but local or regional banks would be more useful in areas where poor education and equally poor communications are problems.

I must say here that the Western world, not only the backward countries, needs education. The prosperous peoples and nations need to be educated into an appreciation of how serious the situation really is.

We of the Western world must realize that in one way or another we have brought millions of people to the point where they know too much to go back to their old life and too little to go on to a new one. We have condemned them, temporarily, to an 'in-between' life, and have unsettled them. To half-educate a man is to make him dangerously malleable in the wrong hands. Education must go all the way. Africans and Indians at open-air cinemas sometimes see Hollywood films about the good life as lived by the lords of the universe, the people of the Western world. These films create many false impressions, but the audiences can see that these people are well fed and that they have many creature comforts. They mean to have these comforts for themselves—at whatever cost. The price for the West and developed world will be no less than that paid by the underprivileged. For instance, the Western peoples will find themselves underprivileged in the evening-out process; under the enormous pressures of population food will become scarcer. Inevitably, too, the conflict already obvious between racial groups will become more acute and dangerous. Some oil-producing countries have withheld oil as a means of applying political pressure; suppose other countries, angry and frustrated, withheld certain types of food? Western nations

115

have already lost much of the respect once paid to them by poorer countries, a factor in the break-up of empires in the 20th century. At its present level, Western affluence is only possible at the expense of the underprivileged nations. When the poorer countries find ways of exploiting this weakness the Western world had better watch out.

Some Western nations need direct education—or at least information—about food values. Barry Commoner, one of the world's leading ecologists from Washington University in St. Louis, notes that the U.S. produces 11,000 calories per person daily [remember that tens of millions of people exist on less than 1,900 calories] but, at the same time, the U.S. is taking thousands of tons of protein-rich anchovies from the Humbolt Current off Peru and Chile. The anchovies are ground up for chicken feed in Arkansas—food energy that could have gone more wisely to human beings. Such inconsistencies probably stem from ignorance.

Athelstan Spilhaus, former Director of Research at New York University and a noted urbanist, estimates that between 1969 and 2000 the U.S. will need to build a family unit for $2\frac{1}{2}$ people every 27 seconds. This would simply accommodate the increase in population and does not take into account the demolition of substandard homes.

Even Americans need to learn that the difference between what is enjoyable in life and what is merely tolerable is narrowing.

9 THE MISERY OF INDIA

I have frequently used India as an example throughout this book, a choice dictated by the simple fact that India is the worst off of all countries, with the possible exception of China. Her people are no hungrier than those of many other countries and her problems are no more acute, but (apart from China) she has more people—550 million, a net increase of 20 million a year—and more problems than other countries. The specious critic might say that she also has a very large area and that, in proportion to size, the problems of, say, Haiti, are just as pressing. This may be so, but the Indian peasant has been the epitome of poverty and suffering for a long time and great numbers do tend to aggravate a problem even if only psychologically. For instance, she has to feed more than 1,700 new mouths every hour. Perhaps there is a psychological basis to the sympathy the world's public seems more ready to accord to the Indian than to any other race. Apart from all this, India's size and numbers make her a major nation, a sort of unofficial spokesman for other poor nations. When India speaks the world should listen.

India is often painted as a lethargic country, but the lethargy is superficial and only thinly covers deep, explosive feeling based on hunger—peasants are sometimes reduced to eating chapattis made from grass—so it is as well to look at some of India's problems not elsewhere stressed in this book.

On the wall of the office of the Indian Home Minister in New Delhi is a large national map bristling with small flags, each representing a town where serious unrest over food has occurred. Some of the trouble is caused by merchants hoarding food, and some by inefficient distribution, but a hungry man rarely looks at causes; he is interested only in effect. As the revolution of rising expectations spreads, many more small flags will appear on the map.

To do all that she must do India needs a lot of money. The economist Barbara Ward believes that India needs foreign assistance to the tune of £400 million a year—and this figure she regards as the absolute minimum. This seems like a lot of money, but is in fact a minute fraction of what the West spends on arms and is equal to about 0.01 per cent of the West's combined national incomes.

Between 1947 and 1970 India had received £2,200 million from the U.S., £900 million from Russia, £300 million from West Germany and £200 million from Britain, but even these vast amounts are inadequate. Mere interest charges on loans can amount to staggering proportions. If India were to borrow 4,000 million dollars from the World Bank she would have to pay back 400 million a year in interest. It could mean that India would need to earmark an impossible 35 per cent of export earnings merely to repay debts. Generous terms must be allowed. A prime example is that of the 50-year no-interest loan made to India for the Damodar Valley project—a major irrigation scheme. This loan, made by the International Development Association—which is managed by the World Bank—requires no repayments between 1962 and 1972. In the second 10 years, 1972–82, capital will be repaid at 1 per cent per year, and the remaining amount at about 3 per cent a year over 30 years. A loan made under these terms allows a country to push ahead with its development programme without the burden of overwhelming debts.

Some critics, economists of repute among them, argue against low-interest loans and gifts of money. Money given freely is spent freely, they say with some justification. A lot of money given without strings has certainly been wasted and some of it misappropriated. The critics say that no money should be lent at less than 8 per cent interest because the Indians have no business becoming involved in any scheme which does not have a return of 8 per cent; if it seems likely to pay less then it should never be started. Having got its 8 per cent the lending agency could return it to be spent on a college or hospital. There is much commonsense in this proposal, but it would severely restrict development, for no educational project could qualify under it for a loan. The best idea would be to allow India to spend the money as she felt best, but to restrict cheque-signing to a member of the bank or lending agency so that some control could be exercised over possible waste.

Petty loans and petty attacks on poverty are nearly useless. An Indian economist, A. N. Agrawal, has observed, 'If the backward agriculture of today is to be transformed into a flourishing agriculture we must give up our policy of nibbling.'

The nibbling Mr. Agrawal refers to are the sporadic and undetermined attempts to raise the output of vegetables and the varieties of millet which include sorghum, bajra and the small black millet which often yields good crops on infertile soils. Improved methods as well as small, local irrigation schemes will help to increase yields. The government did invite Japanese agriculturists to introduce the soya bean and improved methods of rice cultivation, but the results can be seen in only a few small areas—the result of more nibbling.

In ways other than agricultural India has given up a policy of nibbling. She has outlawed 'untouchability' and 'unseeability' in a determined effort to get rid of the caste system, and as part of the largest experiment in social engineering ever attempted. Since the beginning of the 1950s she has been making a sustained effort to modernize her economic structure and to diversify her production and exports. Government planning has centred on major industrial ventures like steel plants, machinery factories and other manufactures. All this is necessary, but history and precedent prove that a country must have a sound rural and agricultural economy before it can hope to build up stable secondary industries.

The tens of millions of people who live in rural districts have no idea what the government is doing. New Delhi and its political machinations are as remote to them as the moon. Even a war fails to excite them. No newspapers reach the villages, and if they did only the schoolteacher—if there is one—the professional scribe and the moneylenders could read them. Most villagers have never even seen a radio, though some have seen films. In the villages life is simple, dull and hard and mealtime is nothing to look forward to, but if a man eats slowly he can give himself the illusion of having a larger meal.

A community is typical only for a region, not for the country as a whole. In the Upper Ganges region, which forms the greater part of Uttar Pradesh, with a population of about 80 million, a typical village has 500 to 5,000 inhabitants, cultivating the surrounding lands of less than 1,000 acres and sometimes of less than 50. The village, a cluster of tiny mud huts, has poor communications with

the outside world, only a few shops and perhaps some crafts-
men.

There is, of course, no doctor, and if somebody becomes
ill he will get better or he will die. No appeal against illness
is possible in a country where no medicines are easily available. A sick person cannot even be given better food or an
extra meal; there is just enough each day to stave off the
worst pangs of hunger. Illness is frequent because hygiene
is poor and the standard of living low. Few families have
anything more than the barest necessities of life, which
means that everybody in the family sleeps on the dirt floor.
Unemployment is one of the inescapable miseries of life,
affecting about a quarter of the population.

Despite reforms introduced since 1954 the small peasants
are still exploited by the large landowners against whom
the village 'council of five'—the panchayat—is usually
powerless. The village may be surrounded by a wall of
dried mud and a strip of land which forms a communal
meadow; in good weather the children spend a lot of time
here, unless the village is lucky enough to have a teacher.
In the Oudh region alone there are nearly 25,000 such villages, which gives some idea of the immensity of problems
of communication, education, administration and distribution.

Delhi, the capital, reflects another side of India. Some of
the city's three million inhabitants enjoy India's highest income—£67·50 yearly against the national average of
£25·50. The capital also has the highest literacy rate—52
per cent. But the gap between rich and poor is as sharply
defined as the railway line which divides them. An acre in
New Delhi houses only 15 Indians, the same area in Old
Delhi is packed with 1,000 people, nearly all unskilled
and unemployed. This is where the street traders flourish.
With charcoal, two stones and a tin plate a man can set himself up selling roasted corn. Girls earn 19p a day carrying
heavy baskets of stones, sand and concrete on building sites.

Half a million people are homeless and so destitute that a piece of abandoned water piping, perhaps three feet wide, is at once grabbed and made into a residence. If a man can find a couple of petrol cans and open them up he has the foundation for a shanty home. Many people cannot find a pipe or a tin can and hire a charcoal stove from a 'street hotel' merely to give themselves an anchor on the pavement. For $2\frac{1}{2}$p a man can buy just enough food at a street hotel to keep his body functioning. Of course, he may have to steal or beg the $2\frac{1}{2}$p. Begging is a hazardous occupation in a city with more than 100,000 beggars.

The situation is so hopeless and so vast that the police leave the pavement dwellers alone provided they do not impede traffic. In winter, when temperatures can drop to the low 40s, the Delhi council opens night shelters. Even then, many people cannot be accommodated in them.

Ten minutes from all this are places like the Ashoka Hotel, where lucky Indians in fabulous costume wait on visitors and tourists. The Ashoka is just a small part of the opulent part of New Delhi, which is typical of many cities with a glittering façade concealing mass misery. With a birth rate of 41.7 per 1,000 against a death rate of 22.8 per 1,000 the misery becomes greater every day.

India's neighbour, Pakistan, has the same daunting problems. The Ganges-Brahmaputra delta area of East Pakistan is especially difficult to administer and this is largely why the people here are vulnerable. In May 1965 a typhoon hit this area, killing about 10,000 people outright. They might have been the lucky ones, for the survivors in hundreds of scattered villages had no food and no fresh water. Two Red Cross launches were able to deliver a little rice and a few mouthfuls of water to some villages but government help was nearly two months in arriving, and by that time other people had died. Seed grain arrived eventually but in many places too late for the growing season. The Red Cross workers distributed water purifying tablets and told the villagers how to use them, but all the time they knew they would use few tablets. These people cannot comprehend the need for water purification,* and apathy caused by hunger would stop them putting such an idea into practice. It is the same apathy that prevents them from going for help and food in an emergency: they simply wait in their villages for somebody to help them. If help does not arrive, they die.

An even worse disaster occurred in November 1970 when a tremendous cyclone devastated an area of 3,000 square miles, leaving 500,000 Pakistanis dead. Virtually all the three million people of the delta suffered. In the face of Pakistani apathy, maladministration and obstruction, foreign aid managed to bring considerable relief to the stricken area but could do nothing to replace the millions of sheep, cattle and goats which had been killed or restore the wrecked fishing fleet.

Of all the problems which bedevil India that of the sacred cow has had most publicity, and something is now being done to lessen their incalculable ravages.

An American, Dr. F. W. Parker, while in India on an official mission was appalled by the 200 million sacred cows roaming the land, dangerously overgrazing the fields, eating food desperately needed for human consumption. Dr. Parker, wondering what could be done to keep down the cow population, read about a new, cheap contraceptive for women, the pliable double-S plastic coil, and reasoned that if it worked for women it should work for cows. After tests in America a pilot project backed by India's Food and Agricultural Ministry was launched in the province of Uttar Pradesh. There has been no protest on religious grounds, and as the cost per cow is only a few pence there is every possibility that fewer cows will be born to increase the ravage of human crops.

Nobody has yet suggested what can be done about the

* A quarter of the world's sick are victims of water pollution.

123

monkeys, sacred as cows to Hindus, which outnumber and out-eat the people of Uttar Pradesh, the most populous state of India.

But India is not hopeless from a livestock point of view. While the cow will long remain sacred, the buffalo is fair game. The City of Bombay has shown what can be done with buffaloes. Bombay had long possessed buffalo dairymen, but they operated in dirty city dairies, the yield was low and the whole business was inefficient. The council moved the dairymen to a thriving estate at Aarey, where 16,000 buffaloes now prosper. Much work was needed, of course, and experts from abroad are still on hand to advise the local buffalo-men about such diverse activities as buffalo-cheese making and artificial insemination. The Aarey scheme triggered off another at Annand, where a co-operative was formed. Both areas now send buffalo milk to a large U.N.I.C.E.F.-equipped processing plant in Bombay, from which the products are distributed to the city. Much of the milk goes, under a council priority system, to poor mothers and small children. What has been done with buffaloes in Bombay can be done elsewhere, though mostly with greater difficulty, for not all local governing groups are as sympathetic and enlightened as that of Bombay.

How are Indian farmers to earn more money so as to be able to buy seeds, fertilizers and tools? The solution must depend on local conditions, but the experience of the state of Uttar Pradesh shows how this may be done. Once again, it was the F.A.O. which inspired the scheme—one to produce hides and skins. As slaughtering is not permitted, the hides and skins came from animals which had died a natural death. This caused complications, but a carcass quick-collection scheme was evolved and drying and tanning centres were set up in villages. Now about 28 drying and 35 tanning centres process and sell about 65,000 hides and skins annually, bringing in a quarter of a million rupees. The project has resulted in a local shoe-making industry and a processing training centre. This could well be an example for other impoverished areas which at present are caught in the vicious poverty-begetting-poverty circle.

Unfortunately, example needs a long time to take effect in India and few schemes, no matter how successful, find emulators. Some model farms, conspicuously prosperous, are as thoroughly ignored now as they were when founded 15 years ago. The dedicated people who run them, including British and American, persevere on the assumption that in the end the Indians' reserve and conservatism will break down.

Meanwhile, although animal products have the greatest nutritional value, in India the average supply of meat per head annually is only two kilograms. But even this figure makes the situation appear rosier than it is; because of extremely uneven distribution millions of people have less than the statistical average.

The traditional sharecropping is another blight on progress. A wealthy landowner may let out his land for a share of the crop—usually 50 per cent. If the hari—the sharecropper—works hard he is resignedly aware that half of his return will go to somebody else. Consequently, he has no incentive to work really hard.

The moneylenders—every village has its usurer—induce the same sort of apathy. Their rates are extortionate, but the peasant farmer has nobody else to whom to turn and within a few years he finds that his life's work is mortgaged to his moneylender. The more he works the more the moneylender takes, so he has no incentive to work hard. The control these men have over Indian village life is as complete as it is merciless. If somebody could establish thousands of small banks to lend money at low rates of interest output would rise—and so would standards of living and optimism.

In the cities some people are better off than the peasants in the country. A friend of mine, a Calcutta schoolteacher,

is well off for India. He is paid £15 a month and so can afford
to give his children two meals a day—at the expense of
having only one meal a day for himself, and a poor meal at
that. Even so, he is better off than the workers in Bombay
textile mills. Here a family man cannot help but overspend
by about £2 a month; he makes up his deficit by borrowing
money from moneylenders at 9 per cent interest and, of
course, is never likely to get out of debt.

The harvest is always a problem. If crops are not devastated by locusts and manage to survive floods and fires and
get their rain at the correct time and somehow produce a
bumper crop, there is another problem: where to put the
grain. In the whole country there are enough efficient storehouses to hold 12 million tons. The rest of the crop is put
into crude dumps, where pests manage to destroy 10 per
cent of the wheat and 20 per cent of the rice.

Hoarding, endemic in a hungry country, is another problem; the poor practise it as well as the rich. It is especially
notable in the Punjab of India, for here, unlike most parts
of India, there is surplus food, so that Punjabi merchants
hoard food in the hope of shortages forcing a price rise.
Public opinion spasmodically demands that hoarders be
punished, but the problem is insoluble. The late Prime Minister, Mr. Shastri, said, 'How can you punish thousands
and millions of people?'

The successful farmer could do much to help increase
India's food production, but he is the man least likely to
do it, because he has the least need to do it. Most Indians
have a cynical attitude to money—if they have enough of
it. They know that traditionally and eternally, somebody
will demand it.

At a U.N. meeting in Holland, in 1970, India's Minister for
Family Planning, Dr. S. Chandra-Sekkar, advanced the
remarkable opinion that good nutrition is the best contraceptive for controlling runaway population growth. Poor
nutrition induced women in countries such as his own to

126

produce from eight to 10 children on the assumption that three would survive to become breadwinning members of the family. If all the children were assured of good nutrition and therefore a reasonable life expectancy mothers would feel freer to have fewer children—or so goes the Chandra-Sekkar theory. And in theory and in an educated society it may work. But Dr. Chandra-Sekhar must also hold the less tenable theory that if the parents are better fed they will be less likely to indulge in sex and less likely to procreate. Most Indian women have a lot of children because they do not know how to stop having them. In many areas of India they have already had critical problems as the result of more money being available. Indian husbands in improved circumstances decided they could afford to have a few *more* children. With the population already increasing by 20 million a year this new attitude is alarming.

Other Indian officials are prone to flights of fantasy about food production. In 1968 some of them were predicting that India would be self-sufficient in food by 1971—which meant that they believed they could feed 70 million more people in 1971 than they could not feed in 1968.

The pros and cons of the birth control controversy, world surpluses, trade agreements, international loans . . . all are beyond eight out of 10 Indians and perhaps it is true that the government would rather the mass stayed ignorant. But not so long ago virtually every Indian was unaware of what went on beyond his village; gradually the news is filtering through to the peasants that hunger is not universal and something that mankind was born to endure. This is the spark which has fired the revolution of rising expectations. That spark is likely to grow into a very big and dangerous fire unless it is damped down with a fairer issue of food and a more satisfying way of life.

In January 1966 a British newspaper correspondent, Gilbert Lewthwaite of the *Daily Mail*, reported that in a remote village near the Nepal border an ill-fed Indian threw himself down and kissed the feet of an American, James Boulware, the agricultural attaché of the American Embassy in New Delhi, while on a field tour. The Indian peasant received half his wages in American-aid wheat, and without it he would have starved to death. No wonder that in his relief he prostrated himself in this act of gratitude.

On the verge of international bankruptcy, India cannot survive without foreign aid, but a difficult problem has arisen. America's readiness to give Indians grain—it is worth £20 a ton, so the gift is considerable—is paling because there is a strong impression that India is becoming too prone to rely on free food and less interested in developing her own agriculture.

In 1957 India needed only 2 million tons of U.S. wheat to sustain her peasants; this was India's own assessment. In 1965 the figure was 6 million; in 1966, 15 million tons. The impression remains, that India is not helping herself as much as she could. The Americans have not reduced their bounty, for the 12 million people herded into relief camps would certainly die—and America would be blamed for letting it happen. This is one of the great dangers of becoming known as a donor nation; if the donations decrease the nation is then reviled.

The U.S. and other donor nations, such as Australia, are reviled anyway, by nationalistic extremists. Some would prefer to have no aid at all. Gilbert Lewthwaite reported that one left-wing M.P. accused the government of 'mortgaging the nation's self respect'. Another said, 'Let us die.'

Fortunately, responsible ministers are more balanced. Replying to the 'Let us die' bravado, the Food Minister suggested that such advocates should be the first to set an example.

Inevitably, the food shortage which follows a drought results in a black market which flourishes despite severe penalties. Still, the racketeers find it difficult to get hold of American wheat, which is marketed directly by the Government, through the 120,000 official shops, which in turn are permitted to supply only 500 registered customers.

In the strength of its prosperity, the West must accept the risks of ingratitude and of recipient countries becoming less self-reliant, but acceptance of the risks does not automatically mean acceptance of the facts and every measure must be taken to ensure that India maintains the dignity of a friend in need and does not become a beggar nation.

One education programme is particularly encouraging. Between them India and the U.S. are to use a space satellite to bring farming information to 20 million people in 5,000 Indian villages. The technology will be American, the programmes Indian. It is recognized that information—on population control as well as farming—can be more efficiently disseminated if semi-literate extension workers do not have to be used. All previous communication systems have been uneconomic and the cost of setting up a network of TV ground stations would be prohibitive. The 'Applications Technology Satellite' will beam programmes direct to antenna-equipped communal TV sets in villages and schools.

Encouraging as this may appear, it should never be forgotten that in the 20 years from 1950 to 1970 the population of India increased by 200 million—little less than the population of the United States; that the annual increase is 20 million—the population of Colombia; and that if birth control plans fail the population will increase to much more than 1,000 million in the year 2000.

10 ASIA'S AGGRESSIVE ATTITUDE

A young lawyer in Manila with whom I have corresponded since he was a student, wrote to me in his youth, 'We Asians are an improvident, fatalistic people and often irresponsible. We have children in large numbers (he was one of a family of 15) but we have no idea how they are to be fed. We do not even think about such a difficulty because most of us know of no way of preventing children from arriving, short, that is, of complete continence, which we are not prepared to accept. To put it as few Asian intellectuals would put it —because of their pride—we need to be protected from ourselves. We want help, but only in some fields will we ask for it. The trouble is that we Asians also cannot look very far ahead. In fact, we do not *want* to look far ahead because the future is frightening. It is enough to look forward hopefully to the next meal. The younger people can dream but with the coming of responsibilities dreams are quickly killed. We do not live, we exist. We cannot enjoy life, we endure it. Those of us who know the West do not hate it in the conventional sense, but we are terribly envious—and acute envy is really an exquisite form of hatred. We Asians can only become hungrier—this is inescapable. Will the West make us even more envious. . . . We won't thank it (the West) for help given—we are too proud for that—but we need help and we know the West can afford to give it, in one way or another.'

This is only part of a poignant letter. The writer had a part-time job as a grave-digger for a few of his student years. His letters about his experiences were moving and anything but entertaining. Once he wrote, 'This week buried a three-year-old who had died of hunger. . . . We asked the father the child's name. He didn't know. He had so many children he couldn't keep the name of all of them in his mind. This does not surprise me; his mind must have been too full of worry. . . . Do you know that in Asia at least half the people now alive will die prematurely because of starvation or malnutrition. If you continue to let this happen, can we Asians forgive you. . . ?'

Much of the Asian attitude to hunger, to over-population and to the West's reaction to these twin troubles is to be found in this young man's comments; his views are the same now that he is older. But Asia's attitude and Asia's problems are even more complex than his expression of them.

At the World Food Congress in Washington in June 1963, the British historian, Professor A. J. Toynbee, warned that there is little hope of winning the fight against hunger without worldwide birth control. He said, 'Today mankind's future is at stake in a formidable race between population growth and famine.' The truth of this sober opinion is no where more in evidence than in Asia. Similarly, in 1965, Dr. Sen warned of widespread famine by 1980. Yet population is still increasing so fast that it throws out of gear every plan for resettlement before it can be implemented.

The Asian is, unfortunately, prolific. By 1986 another 1,000

131

million people could be living in the already over-crowded, underfed countries of Asia—another mass of people to feed, house, clothe, educate—and keep happy. The hunger and poverty and appalling ignorance being suffered by millions of Asians today is nothing compared with 'the hell of to-morrow', as an Asian editorial writer has expressed it.

In 1950 there were 1,317 million Asians; by 1980, according to a United Nations estimate, there will be at least 2,500 million. The biggest increase will be in South-east Asia, where the population is expected to rise from 127 million (the 1950 figure) to 363 million. And this is a most conservative estimate.

It is difficult to grasp the concept of increasing tens of millions; to talk in such numbers blinds one to the facts and problems they contain. The figures mean, for instance that 55 out of every 100 people in the world will be Asians —and yet the whole of Asia comprises about one-sixth of the world's land mass. They mean that 75 people will be living in every square kilometre—whereas only nine people live in the same area in the United States and the Soviet Union.

What brought about this prospect of exploded population? People had more children after the war of 1939–45 and *their* children are having children of their own, but ironically, the problem is the price of progress. Since the war, doctors, engineers and scientists have eradicated many of the causes of death in developing countries. Fewer mothers are dying in childbirth, fewer children die in infancy, fewer people die of disease. Deaths caused by drought and pests, though not eliminated, have been sharply reduced. I use the word 'fewer' relatively, for millions still die of disease.

Science has thus presented Asia with a dreadful dilemma. By 1980 Asia will need to develop fantastically if the people of that year are to enjoy a standard of living comparable to that of the present-day Japanese. Compared with 1960, Asia will need, according to the *Asia Magazine*, at least:

300,000,000 more homes

10,000,000 more hospital beds

120,000 more primary schools with 1,000 pupils to each school

10,000,000 more gallons of water a day

1,000,000,000,000 more kilowatts of electricity annually

82,000,000 more tons of rice annually

10,000,000 more tons of wheat annually

180,000,000 more tons of vegetables annually

60,000,000 more tons of fish annually

13,000,000 more tons of meat annually

5,500,000 more policemen

1,000,000 more firemen

6,000,000 more government officials

On October 22, 1961, the *Asia Magazine* noted that, 'Only through birth control can the mounting problem . . . be contained within manageable limits'. Birth control is discussed elsewhere in this book, but reference to it in connection with Asia is necessary here because the problem is so urgent. Social workers who have conducted surveys in Asia say that many ordinary people living in rural areas are not hostile to the idea of family planning, though it is true that in some villages people are prejudiced against birth control because they cannot be certain how many of their children will survive—and in a land where there are no old-age pensions, children are the only insurance that parents have. But other people are only too well aware of economic pressures on a large family.

Where no family planning is allowed—such as in the Philippines, where the dominant religion is Roman Catholic —the population increase is frightening. The Philippines have the highest rate of population growth in South-east Asia. In 1966 the population was 32 million; in 1970, 37 million; in 1980 it will be nearly 50 million. In other countries where there is little birth control—Ceylon, Thailand,

133

Burma—populations are also mounting rapidly.

By 1980 Indonesia will probably have the fifth largest number of people in the world—behind mainland China, India, Russia and the United States. Coping with the estimated 150 million will be an immense problem, though the difficulty here is not lack of land, but the even distribution of people over it. Java is already greatly overcrowded, but Sumatra is underpopulated.

I have already said that in Mauritius the population explosion is visible. This applies, too, to Hong Kong. In Hong Kong you never stop hearing about land reclamation, naturally an all-pervading topic where many more than 4 million live in a small territory. Eighty per cent of the population are squeezed into 12 square miles of the twin cities of Victoria and Kowloon. Between them they make up the fourth largest city in the British Commonwealth and their narrow confines are the scene of endless combat between man and nature. Man gains transitory victories; nature will win the war.

With many young people reaching marriageable age the impact on the colony's population will be violent, and by the end of the century it should reach 10 million.

By carving apartment sites out of hillsides and dumping the earth into the sea to create level industrial land man is gaining breathing space. Land reclamation is not new to Hong Kong; the main thoroughfare, Queen's Road Central, was once the shoreline. The commercial centre of the city stretching east from there to the sea stands almost entirely on reclaimed land. Hong Kong airport, a promontory a mile long and 800 feet wide, is completely reclaimed from the waters of Kowloon Bay. In fact, Hong Kong has more than 2,000 acres of reclaimed land. Kun Tong township is to have a population of 150,000 on an eventual 500 acres of new land. Interesting and ambitious though this and other projects are they cannot keep pace with the population growth.

It is rewarding but disturbing to study Asia and Asia's attitude to the twin problems of hunger and over population. However, we will omit Japan because this country, discussed in one way or another in several places in this book, has mostly overcome the problems and its people now have an enviable prosperity.

The innocent, naïve way in which the rest of the world manages to ignore Asia is astonishing. It might not exist for all the notice that many people give it. At best, *some* Westerners are interested in *some* part of Asia. This is partly the fault of the Western school system, which devotes little time to Asian affairs. I have studied many school and university text books on Asia. Nearly all have the common defect that they ignore the problems of population and hunger, yet these basic facets of human geography influence every other aspect of geography.

But the general Western attitude to Asia is symptomatic of the 'If we ignore it perhaps it will go away' school of thought.

The *Asia Magazine* says, 'Population—explosive or otherwise—would not be such an insurmountable problem if, with the help and guidance of the U.N., countries pooled their resources, ideas and skilled manpower for the benefit of all'. But there has been no pooling and waste—'the most effective ally of hunger' Dr. Sen calls it—has continued. The waste is rarely wilful in Asia—though God knows it is wilful enough in other parts of the world—but this is no consolation. At least 15 per cent of Indonesia's food production is lost through waste resulting from lack of processing and storage. This is a technical factor. There are other, more general factors barring the way to greater food production in Asia. Among these are land tenure systems that permit the farmer little incentive to work more intelligently or vigorously, high rents and inefficient marketing structures.

Then there is ignorance about food preparation. One of

135

the first things that an F.A.O. team found when it visited Burma was that the nutritive value of much of the rice there was badly impaired. Customarily, rice is washed thoroughly and then boiled in an excess of water. When the water is poured off, thiamine, a vitamin in which rice is rich, is poured off, too.

Surveys also showed that the Burmese diet was poor in animal protein, calcium and Vitamins A and C. Certain social habits barred nursing mothers from eating vegetables, fruit, eggs, milk and sugar. Pulses of various kinds, which are excellent sources of protein, were an important export commodity, but were disliked and eaten only in limited amounts by the Burmese. F.A.O. teams set up displays and exhibits, but only a minute percentage of the people was able to see them and to benefit from them. Goodwill is not enough when it comes to reaching and impressing millions of illiterate people.

Asia is an area of many tensions, complexes, ideologies and frustrations, but one stands out above all. Impatience. Asia is more restive than South America, more inflammable, more impatient. The impatience growing throughout Asia is one of the most dangerous aspects of the continent. It shows itself in the periodical riots which afflict every Asian country from Korea to Indonesia. It is no coincidence that the rioters are usually young people and mostly students at that. Though emotionally and politically immature, they are not naturally violent and reactionary. They are no different, basically, from young people in other parts of the world, yet their impatience has caused much violence and change in Asia in recent years. Nothing happens quickly enough to suit most thinking people—and young people have been taught to think.

Older people may not riot, but they, too, are impatient, for human and understandable reasons. During the colonial days, not long departed, many Asians mistakenly believed that their countries were rich. They saw some foreign firms being obviously successful in some aspects of local industry. The representatives of these firms had fine offices and homes, lived well and periodically loaded a ship with rice, rubber, tea, timber or some other commodity. The natives of the countries can be forgiven for thinking that the 'riches' of their nations were great and inexhaustible. The bitter reality is that resources are much smaller per head than in the West, although the gross product might be large. For instance, Malaya is the wealthiest country of Asia in proportion to population, but its production per head is only a fifth that of the U.S. Indonesia, in most years the poorest country, has an annual income only 2.5 per cent that of the U.S.

When the Asian countries threw off colonial domination, whether it was benevolent or not, they formed their own governments and waited expectantly for the miracles which they *knew* came with independence. The minor miracles duly happened—the new countries were given seats in the United Nations, they produced a national flag and probably an airline. Everybody was very pleased for a time and they sat back to wait for more miracles. Most of them are still waiting, unable to solve the mystery of why countries once rated as priceless by colonial powers should now be poor and backward.

It is a mere truism that the longer a man waits for something the more questions he begins to ask himself. And every impatient Asian asks particularly, 'If a man wants to be rescued from unjust traditions, from poverty, from suffering and distress, can political ideologies offer the solution?'

One difficulty is that the planning, the thinking, the administration of every village, town and city is in the hands of a small group. No matter how sincere and dedicated this group might be, progress tends to be limited and ideas to become muffled.

These are the main problems worrying Asian leaders:

The disparity between ancient rural practices and the

137

up-to-the-minute modernity of cities and industrial areas.

How to find sufficient food for the urban and residential areas as changing forms of land tenure and improving dietary standards cause surpluses to dry up.

The difficulty—probably the impossibility—of absorbing the pressure of population solely by domestic developments.

The nagging apprehension that increasing industrialization will produce greater strain rather than relief.

Bridging the wide, deep gulf between the ancient, traditional facets of Asian economy and modern theory and practice.

The worry of keeping the common people fed well enough, and therefore reasonably content, until the expected miracles can be created.

The many difficulties present in attempting to amalgamate plural societies into a single nation. Some Asian countries are, in effect, groups of widely differing tribes rather than an homogeneous people. Even the more progressive countries, such as Malaya, Thailand and the Philippines have large ethnic groups who certainly do not consider themselves part of a nation, since they have no conception of nationhood.

Finally the problem of checking population growth until some sort of salvation can be evolved.

Few people of the Western world appreciate or have sympathy with the dilemma facing sincere Asian politicians. To give their people more food and better standards generally they must raise some money by direct taxation—but the people are already highly taxed. They desperately want to improve the standard of living but must spend so much money abroad on capital equipment that, for a time at least, living standards must drop. The politicians must make the ordinary people believe in government and administration, but in the process the people come to believe that the government is some sort of benevolent big brother who will provide all. Then they are disillusioned when they have no more to eat than before. This is when Communism begins to appeal, for democracy in the midst of poverty is a ridiculous contradiction.

Democratic government needs a certain human climate in which to thrive. In Asia democracy faces complex difficulties. It unduly raises the expectations of the people, but it cannot effectively mobilize human and material resources for rapid development—not as effectively, anyway, as Communism can mobilize them. Political democracy cannot exist in Asian countries for any length of time unless it provides for rapid economic growth. When the countries of Asia attained independence the forces that led to throwing off the foreign yoke were channelled towards higher standards of living, full employment at living wages, full opportunity for human development, reduction of inequalities in income and wealth distribution and various welfare improvements. Welfare concepts and hopes were even written into constitutions.

The inability of governments to satisfy ambitious economic objectives is partly due to the very narrow economic base on which Asian countries have had to build. A country dependent on one or two commodities does not have much room for manoeuvre. People of the various Asian countries are not prepared to give the necessary time to their governments, because they do not understand the process of economic development. They think there are short cuts to development and that rapid economic growth is possible without sacrifices. They are disillusioned and frustrated.

Successful democracy demands that the people should have the time and means to participate in government to some degree. But most Asians cannot participate; the toil for daily food leaves them no energy for such distractions. Also, the people must have some economic security and prosperity at stake in a democracy; they are unlikely to

fight for a democracy in which they have no such investment. More opportunity for the people to share in growth
is needed, if only to stimulate their interest in economic
goals.

The elected government hesitates to impose necessarily
hard measures on an illiterate and unimaginative electorate,
on whose support it must rely. It is just about impossible to
prove to such people any relationship between present sacrifice and future reward.

Most Asian countries have pinned their faith on economic
planning, but for planning to succeed, there must be general
agreement on basic questions, or a lot of effort will be
wasted. There are dangers in democratic planning and the
necessary economic control must be balanced against freedom. The objective should be the minimum of control and
direction and the least interference with individual freedom,
consistent with attaining rapid growth. Wherever democracy
has collapsed in South-east Asia, the cause was not the inroads made on freedom by planning, but the failure of the
democratic government to tackle the economic problem in
a determined way.

Planning implies unified control, and decisions based on
a total view of the economy mean that in all planning, democratic or totalitarian, the state must play a dominant role,
hence the need for a government that will refuse to com-
promise its principles and will not buy popularity. One way
towards stable democracy is a quick building up of a surplus
economy to ensure that the people have a certain minimum
of material comforts. And investment must be made not only
in machinery but in the skills, health and education of the
people.

The increasing growth of population makes difficult the
task of keeping up even the low existing standards. That
certain basic conditions for rapid economic growth seem to
be lacking or are inadequate complicates the situation. First,
without reasonable political stability, it is not easy to quick-

en the pace of development. Second, there is the lack of an adequate supply of private enterprise that cannot be quickly compensated for by government or public enterprise. Third, trained administrative, technical and business personnel are in short supply. Finally, because of the cultural time-lapse between the traditional and the modern, the poorly educated people do not comprehend what functions and duties they should perform to gain an adequate standard of living. These handicaps have slowed the growth of economic development in Asian countries to a pace too slow to keep up with population increases. Before any Asian country can stand on its own feet economically, the population climb must be slowed.

Everywhere throughout Asia foreign money is helping countries to balance their budgets. (See the chapter—Trade and Aid.) Some nations have had to swallow their pride; others are unashamedly holding out their hands for offerings. But whether the assistance is grudgingly or readily accepted, the picture is the same—foreign aid is keeping the developing countries solvent. For nearly every Asian nation this state of affairs is inevitable. To maintain economic progress, let alone increase it, capital must be poured into the treasuries. But to many people the words 'foreign aid' are ugly, even frightening. People see foreign aid transactions as selling a nation's soul to the devil. There is something in this, for it is difficult for a struggling country not to be obliged to sell part of its political independence. More sensitive Asians feel that there is little difference between outright, physical colonialism and indirect economic colonialism.

The younger generation, represented by the articulate students, are nationalistic and when something is offered 'for nothing' they want to know what strings are attached.

How long is foreign aid going to last? I believe that if it goes on too long some Asian countries will develop a foreign-aid mentality—that of a drug addict unable to exist hap-

141

pily without an injection. An even more pertinent question is this: are the majority of the people getting any benefit from foreign aid? A large proportion of the money is spent on paying for armies which would be utterly useless in a serious conflict, on balancing an unreal and shaky last year's budget and on buying valuable machinery and equipment that lies idle for years and turns rusty because too few trained people are avilable to operate it.

Asian governments have been unable to resist status symbols—always costly luxuries. The most pathetically ridiculous is the national airline symbol. Every country, large or small, has its own national airline, but even the most modern, best-equipped and wealthiest international airlines sometimes find it difficult to meet costs. An airline is tremendously expensive to run and most Asian countries lose heavily on their obsolete aircraft, though they manage to hide their losses under the complicated figures of balance sheets.

Somehow, Asian countries—like those of Africa, South and Central America—must be shown that arrant, unreasoning nationalism has frightened away individual businessmen and has made large foreign firms wary about building and investing in such countries. The risk of having an industry or a company nationalized is too great. This was shown in Ceylon, from which—following a policy of nationalization —many British tea and rubber planters exported much of their profits and capital to East Africa, where new tea plantation areas were opened up. These plantations were soon competing with Ceylon for the traditional markets. In effect, Ceylon, dependent on tea exports for 60 per cent of her income, had created her own competition. This was nationalism gone mad. Some nations discourage foreign capital— and then seek help, in the shape of loans and aid, from outside. It would be healthier to encourage foreign investment.

Sicco L. Mansholt, leading agricultural expert in the Common Market, sees a solution to the Asian problem in trade, not in aid. He told the World Food Congress that to begin with, the U.S. and Europe must agree to give the under-developed countries special trade benefits—guaranteed prices, guaranteed markets, low tariffs. 'If we want to help,' he said, 'we must make it possible for the underdeveloped to sell their products to us. We must not give them hand-outs, but the chance to produce, to develop their industries and to sell to us. . . . Until we do we should shut our mouths about aid to the hungry.'

Another danger is that Asian towns and cities are ex-panding dangerously—dangerously because they are not or-ganized to cope with such rapid absorption of people who cannot be fitted into the country areas. Slums result—and slums are notorious breeding places of intellectual and poli-tical unrest. The tensions of the cities of Asia can be felt, seen and sensed, as any observant Western visitor knows. The instability is due, very often, to empty bellies and im-possible domestic and social stresses.

Vast numbers of people do not even have clean, pure water to drink. Often, I have seen the same stream used for bathing, washing clothes, waste disposal and drinking. This is commonplace in nearly every country of Asia. Possibly three-quarters of the population have unsafe water to drink; water-borne diseases affect many millions of people annually and in South-east Asia kill at least a million—apart from the 2 million who die each year in India from the same cause.

There are bright spots in the Asian problem. In Laos, Cambodia and Thailand rice continues to increase in acre-age and production, but not as fast as the population sup-plied by these sources. In any case, in Burma rice production has substantially decreased and is less than two-thirds that of 1938. Rice is no longer the chief item among export values in Indo-China.

Escapists might suggest that the internal food and popu-lation problems will produce wars among the Asian coun-tries and they will see in these wars a form of solution to the problem—a solution akin to the Nazis' self-satisfied solv-

143

ing of the 'Jewish problem'. Wars there already are and others might well occur, but they cannot solve the hunger problem, for even less food is produced when a country is ravaged by war. Those who survive the wars and the consequent famines will be even more bitter—and the birth rate would soon restore the numbers to normal and then continue to advance.

The Indian poet Rabindranath Tagore, whose centenary was celebrated in 1961, suggested one solution to city dwellers of Asia: 'Take each of you charge of some village and organize it. Educate the villagers and show them how to put forward their united strength. Look not for fame or praise. . . . Do not expect even the gratitude of those for whom you would give your life, but be prepared rather for their opposition.'

This is more profound than it is cynical, and Western nations and people should take note of it.

The Americans nearly always plainly mark each sack of food as coming *From the people of the United States.* They have publicized it as the 'best-known food label in the world'. I am not sure that such flamboyant publicity is sound practice. Many a simple-minded peasant reasons that Americans must indeed be very well fed if they can afford to give away food, so what sacrifice is it to them to hand him a bag of grain? It is the old American complex of wanting to be thanked for doing a good deed. All that matters is that hungry people should be fed; they will then become more moderate, less Communist-minded. Some individuals may have a deep enough sense of gratitude to kiss the shoes of a visiting American (see previous chapter), but the great majority of people would do no such thing. In any case, do not let us be hypothetical about all the donated food. In the case of the U.S., it is cheaper to ship some surplus food abroad than it is to store it. And normal agricultural exports have increased by the same amount as food aid.

The Asian is not only impatient, he is perplexed, especially if he can read or has the opportunity to hear at second-hand from other people who can read. He knows, for instance, that nearly every home in America has at least one motor car and that many have two; that every Swedish housewife has a washing machine; and that nearly every British family has a television set. To the average person, these are the signs of progress—and the Asian wants them. But herein lies a conflict, for the Asian idealists wonder if they want this kind of progress when it appears to bring in its train such disturbing side effects. These thinkers note that America, for all her affluence, still has a serious racial problem and appalling slums; that Sweden has the highest suicide rate in Western Europe, and that Britain is beset with labour problems and juvenile delinquency.* They admit that the example of the more developed countries has provided an incentive and a goal but they are worried that in trying to achieve conventional progress they are sacrificing their own cultures and tradition. This is a further cause for resentment against the West.

Indonesia, Burma, Vietnam, Thailand and the Philippines are all trying different methods of avoiding the undesirable by-products of progress. Some seem strange to people inside and outside Asia, but it is almost impossible to understand the problems of the developing nations in clear black and white.

'Solutions' include banning teen-agers from seeing American, Swedish, Italian and French films; forbidding the sale of clothing felt to be provocative or indecent; discouraging co-educational schools. In all these countries censorship of a type is practised, to eliminate from magazines and newspapers any reference to 'immoral Western practices and trends'—such as juvenile delinquency, sexual equality,

---

* Japan has not only made an incredible leap forward industrially and commercially; she has also deteriorated morally, socially and perhaps culturally. She, too, has a high suicide rate, many slums, acute tensions resulting from the pace of living.

homosexuality, drug-taking. Many responsible Asians deplore the influence of pop music and many records are banned. Even coffee bars are considered to have an adverse and corrupting influence. In South Korea teen-age schoolgirls have been forbidden to wear high-heeled shoes, make-up, and skirts too high or necklines too low. This new, almost puritanical mood has swept Asian capitals.

On top of all this the Asian attitude is influenced by the realization that Asian countries now have considerable bargaining power. Parts of Asia—collectively the areas that comprise Monsoon Asia—were for a long time merely distant estates of Western powers. Now these countries find themselves the focus of external pressures from the Western democracies and from Russian or Chinese Communism. After almost total eclipse for four centuries the leaders of the new nations find their countries with major importance in international affairs. They are aware of their consequent influence, and of the fact that the military security of the globe depends for many reasons on parts of the Oriental world.

As a leading writer on Asian affairs, E. H. G. Dobby, has noted, 'Transport, communications and the huge numbers of people in Asia make the zone a fulcrum of international political and economic power, causing to some extent a dwarfing of the Western world. . . . Popular education, literacy, the radio and the aeroplane are restoring Asians to knowledge, removing them from twilit faith into the stark facts which present problems . . . alarming in the size . . . but reassuring at second examination because they are problems of a kind already known elsewhere, and because their size means that they offer fields of activity which could keep fully employed the whole of the world's people and resources for several generations.'*

There is an undercurrent of hope in Mr. Dobby's views, but it is one I cannot share because not the whole of the

* *Monsoon Asia*, University of London Press.

146

world's people are interested in the problems of Asia. And though the problems might be known elsewhere this does not, in itself, help the Asians to master the problems.

Nearly all writers who have studied the food and population problems completely ignore China, presumably because it is difficult to know how to help or handle her. Indeed, it is virtually impossible to help China, but a country of 800 million people cannot be ignored. Giving aid to China is a peculiarly complex problem. Whatever aid could be given would be a minute fraction of the aid needed; the Chinese would permit no supervision or check on disbursement of aid. They generally refuse to accept aid, and as a Communist country they do not, in the eyes of most governments, qualify for it. Reaching the Chinese with counter-propaganda is also an impossible task. The great bulk of Chinese are illiterate and have no radios and in any case it would be simple for the authorities to stop any attempts at informing the people about outside affairs.

Some observers have suggested that outside aid to China, on a scale comparable to that given to Taiwan—where even peasants are relatively prosperous—would produce an equivalent standard of living. They have not examined figures closely enough. A sum of £3,000 million would be needed annually, which is beyond any group of nations to provide. Also, for many reasons, the economic situations in the two countries cannot be compared. Even Loren Fessler, who knows as much as anybody about the situation in China, concedes that, 'There is no ready solution to the dreary problem. . . .' And he adds that the resulting frustrations in this 'dangerous invalid among nations' constitute a threat to international peace.

The self-opinionated West might not wish to admit it but it could learn something from Chinese farming methods —not perhaps to put into practice in Western countries but further to develop the backward countries. In recent years the Chinese, finding that irrigation and drainage, threshing,

147

tilling and the processing of harvested crops made the greatest demands on manpower, gave close attention to improved equipment for these tasks. They have since produced, among other things, diesel motors, threshers, various crop-processing machines, walking tractors, hand sprayers, animal-drawn three-bladed hoes, seed drills, rubber-tyred carts and farm trailers. Scores of mechanization experiments are in progress. The smaller 8 h.p. diesel motors made by the Hupeh Provincial Diesel Engine Plant have been particularly useful in fighting waterlogging and drought and perhaps 120,000 are in use. These motors have many uses. They drive specially designed machines for threshing, husking, milling, pressing, cotton-ginning, tea-rolling, flax- and hemp-breaking, peanut-shelling, potato-powdering and corn-cobbing.

China has, in fact, achieved some astonishing successes since 1949. For instance, in that year the rice yield was only 48.6 million tons. By 1954 it had reached 70.9 million tons and is now more than 450 million tons. Wheat has increased, too, from a mere 13.8 million tons in 1949 to an estimated 205 million tons at present—in a non-drought year.

Other production is increasing greatly, but it remains true that countless millions of Chinese are underfed.

Food is a totally absorbing subject in mainland China. In time of famine a month's rice ration barely lasts three days. As recently as 1965 sugar was issued only four times a year and even today women try to thicken watery soup by adding grass. Village life in China is a constant struggle for physical survival—survival of the strongest, the most cunning and the most hard-hearted. Loren Fessler says that by Western standards life is so utterly harsh as to seem not worth living.

But the Chinese are trying. In 1968 they made about 7 million tons of fertilizer and they bought other supplies from Japan and Europe. They even bought several complete production plants and developed many small plants to produce fertilizer for local use.

Despite improvements in grain crops, China imports wheat from Canada, Argentina and Australia. Apart from increasing internal supplies of grain, the result is to release large areas for production of other crops and is permitting larger exports of rice, which bring a higher price on world markets.

Chinese trade is likely to be hampered for some time by a shortage of foreign exchange. Demands for capital equipment under the current Five-year Plan can be met only if exports can be increased. The bulk of Chinese exports consists of agricultural products, textiles and cheap consumer goods for which Hong Kong is the chief outlet.

China lacks sufficient cultivable land to feed the ever-increasing numbers. In all, only 10 to 15 per cent of the area can now be used for farming. The hard fact is that China has probably 275 million acres of arable land, which means that about half an acre is available for each peasant who lives on and from the land. The rest of the country is too steep, too dry, too high or too exhausted. In 2 million square miles of China survey units and camel caravans can travel for days and meet nobody, for 90 per cent of the inhabitants live in the eastern third of the country, especially in the Yangtze valley, an area of 435,000 square miles which holds about 380 million people. Every year hundreds of thousands of people are sent to the west to ease the pressure in the east.

But no developments could possibly keep pace with the rising population, which should reach 1,000 million by 1980. China is vulnerable to famine at the best of times and as the population goes up by the tens of millions so the magnitude of each catastrophe increases proportionately. Millions of Chinese will certainly die of hunger but even this wastage cannot check the national increase. Eventually the Chinese must spill over in some direction.

Chinese propaganda, readily available in the West, makes great play with information, both true and false, about food. The Chinese propaganda experts tell their own people, as

149

they tell those of other nations, that the people of the West, while well-fed themselves, deliberately make sure that other races remain hungry, knowing that hungry men cannot be efficient soldiers. They propound the theory that many of China's problems have been caused by Western imperialism. Even the lack of food, they say, is partly due to the old colonial powers having prevented China from developing her agrarian reforms. One of the worst aspects of the flood of propaganda is that the U.S. is accused of neo-colonialism through the food and money she distributes to the underdeveloped or developing countries. This is particularly dangerous because the peoples who receive American bounty are apt to believe this approach and will therefore resent American aid even more than they do now. Other donor nations, such as Britain, Germany, Canada and Australia are accused of the same sort of 'crimes', but special viciousness is reserved for the U.S. The propaganda contains innuendoes, and sometimes even outright statements, that donated food has been condemned for human consumption in the United States, but that it is considered suitable for Asians; or that it contains a sophisticated drug likely to impair male potency and female fertility so that Asians will have fewer children. The idea is, according to this line of propaganda, that in a decade or two Asian nations will be softened up and ripe enough for take-over by the United States in her devious attempts to gain world domination. Responsible, educated people in Asian countries ignore all this unfounded nonsense, but hot-headed students are apt to repeat it with an attitude of 'There must be something in this', while millions of peasants, having had it read to them by local agitators, swallow it whole.

In a way, one can admire China's sense of independence, but it is a great pity that China and the West are unable to co-operate. Both could benefit from what each has learnt for, make no mistake, China, under the desperate impetus of having to feed such vast numbers of people, has learnt a great deal that could be used in other parts of the world. She is not the ignorant giant that many Westerners suppose. Similarly, the West could teach China a great deal in production of food and non-production of human beings.

One of the great challenges of history is for the West to concentrate on producing miracles of agricultural technology, nuclear development or synthetic-food to achieve a solution to the China problem. What happens in the world's most populous country during the next few years can be of vast importance to the rest of the world.

But if China herself cannot appreciably be reasoned with or helped, her propaganda abroad can be countered. It is still said that money talks; but food has an even louder voice. The Chinese propaganda which permeates Asia (and parts of Africa and South America) can be nullified by giving the peoples of Asia enough to eat. There are many subtle ways in which the 'poisoned and condemned food' propaganda could be countered.

E. H. G. Dobby asks the question, 'Have we to expect a great march of hungry hordes from Monsoon Asia to emptier places in Australia, Central Asia and Africa?' He does not answer his own question, but his mere posing of it suggests that such a thing is possible and that it has exercised his mind. I believe that it is probable. Even more probable is a growing hate by the Asians for everything that the West stands for. It will be a blind, not a reasoning hate, for it will be based on only one fact—'*They* have plenty to eat; we do not'. Poverty and hunger are no longer regarded as inevitable or evils to be tolerated.

The problem is fantastically difficult, but as each year passes it can only become more difficult, so that the time to start on it is now. The economic health of the West is in danger if Asian people remain cut off from general human circulation and from fair and proportionate use of the world's commodities.

One sobering thought remains. If nuclear warfare is unleashed it will be directed at the industrialized and urban nations with great and perhaps total destruction of their industry and their organization. Most Asian nations have no military installation worth knocking out and little industry that could be turned to warlike channels. In any case, destruction of their cities would serve no purpose, unlike the ruin of Western cities. So the Asians of the tiny farms, the millions and millions of peasant subsistence or near-subsistence farmers and their urban cousins will be the dominant surviving group. Dominant, will they want to dominate? Will they seek the opportunity to take what they need? Will they show charity to others when relatively little has been shown to them?

11   FISHING; FISH FARMING; FOOD FROM THE SEA; POLLUTION

Professor Ritchie Calder, one of the most militant and energetic food specialists, has observed that in our use of the sea's food potential we are still at the cave-man stage, 'hunting the sea creatures instead of husbanding them'.

Scientists all over the world have begun to appreciate the tremendous importance of the great sheets of water and to concede that men, before too long, must obtain most of his food, minerals, fresh water and energy from the sea. The danger is that the seas will be as irresponsibly exploited as the land has been. They should be cultivated and developed, but before this can happen intensive, extensive and expensive research must be undertaken. So far, only the Soviet Union has shown enough interest in the work and is clearly in the lead in oceanography. The Soviet has well over 100 ships and several submarines exclusively engaged in ocean research. The race to control the oceans, to tame them and use them is a prime factor in national survival.

But it is not only with sea creatures that the human race is still at the cave-man stage; only a few countries have begun to exploit the oceans for food other than fish, such as seaweed.

The sea could probably support 100 times the amount of food on land. The whole human race could be fed from the seas—the last food source on earth—if they could be scientifically farmed. But already man is dumping radio-active waste into the sea and this could lead eventually to chaos and destruction.

There are three aspects to use of the sea to provide food —normal fishing, fish farming, marine-growth farming. Except in isolated instances, not even conventional fishing is efficiently carried out and the scope in all three is so tantalizingly great as almost to beggar the imagination.

About 52 million tons of food, including fish and raw materials, are taken from the sea annually. Obviously, this is a minute proportion of what is potentially available. As long ago as 1940, with oceanography in its infancy, Professor August Krogh of Denmark estimated that each cubic metre of sea water contains 1.5 grams of protein and 3.9 grams of carbohydrates in the form of plankton. The world food problem would be solved if the plankton could be harvested and concentrated; it is a very big 'if' at the moment, but it must eventually be achieved.

The sea is virtually untouched as a food source, for although a large quantity of fish is caught, fish farming has a long way to go as an industry, even though many villages in Thailand, Madagascar, Burma and Java make great use of it. For conventional fishing the southern hemisphere, 81 per cent water, is unexploited and provides only 2 per cent of the world's marketed fish. Yet the southern hemisphere has many poor nations.

The edible portion of the catch amounts to only nine pounds per person a year, less than 1 per cent of the human diet. This is out of proportion; there is much more water than

154

land on the earth's surface yet nearly all man's food comes from the land. Tragically, almost all countries suffering from serious and chronic protein deficiency border seas where fish are plentiful.

Properly managed, the oceans could become the world's richest suppliers of food. Earth food is limited to a few inches in depth; the oceans could be cultivated to great depths and production in depth is vital to secure the quantities of food we are going to need.

The herring fisheries of the world, wisely and more competently handled, could produce much more than at present. An average female herring deposits at least 30,000 eggs each season and could produce as many as 250,000 in her lifetime. As there are apparently three females to every male, the overall potential is enormous. But for many reasons only the tiniest fraction of the number of eggs hatch and reach maturity. If the eggs could be protected the herring harvest could be vastly increased from the world total of about 9,000 million pounds.

But if the fish yield from traditional fishing areas—notably the North Sea and Icelandic waters, off Newfoundland, off Japan—can be increased, the possibilities are even greater off Africa, Asia, Australia and South America.

For centuries men have been fighting for cultivable land. But only in recent years have fishing wars started. Hasn't anybody appreciated the significance of this? The Koreans have fought the Japanese; the Americans the Peruvians; the British the Icelanders; the Brazilians the French and so on. These conflicts point to the growing importance of fish.

Russia's catches are constantly increasing. Off Newfoundland Russian fishermen are taking 10 times more fish than local fishermen. They are taking large quantities off the coasts of Japan and South Africa and are now operating in the middle of the Indian Ocean. Between 1954 and 1967 the Russian trawler fleet increased fivefold and today she has the world's largest and most modern seagoing fishing fleet.

The Russian fish submarines are small and fast and carry a crew of only three. Working in pairs, they stalk a shoal of fish already located by helicopter.

The helicopter co-pilot, who happens also to be a marine biologist, can tell from his sonar readings the depth, size and density of the shoal. The Russians are using helicopters in the Caspian Sea, the Black Sea and the Sea of Azov, as well as in the great oceans.

Co-operating with the helicopter, the submarines prepare for the catch. A big nylon net, linking the two submarines, unfolds behind them as the submarines move to either side of the shoal. They then surface, towing their catch to a factory ship which sucks the fish aboard and, in some cases, immediately processes them. This idea, evolved by Lev Senkyevitch and generously backed by the Kremlin, is yet another reason why the Russians are doing so well in fishing. Another reason is that the Kremlin ordered that every fishing boat must be equipped with sonar gear. Many fishermen of other nations, even after years of publicity and example, are still not convinced of the effectiveness of sonar.

Other countries could profit greatly by copying Russian methods. In the Caspian, for instance, fishermen were dissatisfied with their net-hauls, so on the advice of oceanographers they now use strong floodlights to attract shoals of certain fish at night. As the fish approach they are drawn by suction into the ships. The catch is now four times greater than before.

Probably the most hopeful method of fishing is the electric 'net' evolved by the Germans, Han Rump and Karl Ulrichs. With their first test the Germans eliminated all scepticism about their 'electrotaxis' methods. The process is simple: an electrode with an impulse of up to 20,000 amperes is let down into the water and fish within a radius of 80 feet are attracted to it, to be drawn into a suction pipe where they are killed by stronger electric shock. The method works well in the open seas—fishing by electricity in lakes and rivers is not new—and a boat can take in 2,000 lbs. of fish in a minute. Apart from other advantages, fishermen normally working under arduous, extreme and dangerous conditions, can now catch in five minutes what they would formerly take in two hours. A further benefit of electrotaxis is that it can be so adjusted that young fish can be kept away from it.

Dr. C. E. Lucas, director of the Fisheries research Laboratories in Aberdeen, believes that fish can be lured into nets or pipes by using chemicals and so far experiments, largely with salmon, confirm his theory. When marine biologists know what chemicals certain fish will follow it will be a simple matter to lay a trail to lead them to stationary suction fish-dredges.

Nevertheless, there is relatively little future for conventional ocean fishery. Of the estimated annual organic production of the world sea—400 thousand million tons—fishery now takes only 52.4 million tons. Although the catch doubled in the decade 1960–70, it is still trifling. Fishery has no effect on world starvation, and can have none in the future. It is merely hunting. Ashore we exchanged hunting for agriculture thousands of years ago. Now it is time to end sea hunting and begin fish farming; today's seafood industry must use its money to enter aquaculture.

Great things can happen in the Indian Ocean, a thick protein concentration surrounded by half-starved nations. In the Persian Gulf many people have never tasted seafood, yet delicious oysters seem undisturbed on the shallow floor, and rich shrimp grounds are being developed for export. In diving-saucer voyages on the continental shelf of the Indian Ocean, Captain Jacques-Yves Cousteau's men have come upon miles of crustaceans almost obscuring the sea floor. A poor country like India, surrounded by productive ocean, might lift itself by diverting agricultural labour to pisciculture.

Today sea-weed is harvested to a limited extent for additives to processed food like ice cream. One of the more promising crops for sea farms is giant kelp, the redwood tree of the ocean. Off California it grows to 300 feet tall, its surface fronds spreading 200 feet wide. Kelp assimilates and stores iodine, potassium and other nutrients. It attracts many fish. It is the fastest-growing plant on earth, with fronds lengthening two feet a day. It is a cold water lover and thrives in man's filth, sewage, soda ash and starchy acids. Today floating reapers behead the Californian kelp forests to make cattle cake. By the turn of the century kelp culture may be a thriving branch of marine agriculture.

Ocean fish farming will have its own inverted form of irrigation, as nuclear-powered blowers on the cold, deep bottom force up nutrition into the poorer surface layers. Chemical nutrients will also be introduced to the fish ranch. The ranch hands will have sea jeeps, miniature submarines, and remote underwater television to keep an eye on things. There are already a dozen underwater natural conservatories protected from fishermen, explosions and pollution. They can be converted into test farms now.

We need not look for radical departures in exploiting the sea; the models of aquaculture exist today, most of them in Japan. There, in the Inland Sea, oysters are cultivated in hanging farms. Cast and spun concrete floats—as many as 6,000 in one place in Kesennuma Harbour—hold up oyster wires from six to 25 feet long. There may be 200 wires to a float and 18 dozen oysters to a wire. The bivalves do not touch the bottom, where pollutants pool and predators, like the starfish, lurk. In Chiba there are abalone ranches, in Mutsu Bay scallop farms. In Okachi Bay the Japanese are raising salmon and trout in huge sleeves of pipe frame and netting, anchored ten fathoms deep. They have feeding chutes from the surface and free divers as farm hands.

158

The Seto Inland Sea Marine Stock Farms Association, incorporated in 1963, runs four large ocean farms, including one at Kamiura which comprises 70,000 square metres. Japan is training her commercial fishermen as divers, to make the transition from sea hunting to sea husbandry.

Farming fish will depend on a tremendous increase in basic research in marine biology. At the same time, water pollution must be curbed. The continental shelf, the best populated, most accessible area is being poisoned at a quickening rate. Dr. David Bellamy of Durham University has shown the catastrophic effect of pollution on sea-weeds, the base of the marine life pyramid, on the coast between Blyth and Middlesbrough. A hundred years ago 97 species of ocean vegetation flourished on this littoral. In a century of industry, filthy effluents from mines, furnaces, chemical plants and cities killed off 56 types. Of those that survive, there are only 11 useful species alive.

British fish scientists have certainly made a start on sea-fish farming and in one way are perhaps even more ambitious than the Russians: they plan to produce fish of a standard size and weight to simplify the equipment for cutting and processing the fish for packaging and for conversion into fish fingers.

They have enclosed about five acres of sea off the Argyll coast in Scotland. This pilot plot fences off an arm of the sea and it will provide information about the conditions needed for rearing fish. The tragedy is that all this information is already known in other countries, and if international co-operation were developed as well as it should be there would be no difficulty in obtaining it. Other sites suitable for fish farms around the British Isles have been surveyed and total an area of 2,000 acres capable of supporting 15,000 fish to the acre or 30 million fish in all. Scientists have already succeeded in hatching and rearing plaice at the Maine Laboratory in Lowestoft on the east coast of England, and other experiments are being made on the Isle of Man. The British White Fish Authority has financed Strathclyde University to carry out research work on fish farming, so Britain is at least in the race.

New fishing grounds are continually being located, and fish are being found at greater depths than previously thought possible.

In 1957 a merchant ship in the Arabian Sea encountered such enormous quantities of dead fish that it was estimated that *en masse* they equalled the total annual world catch. The fish were probably killed by a build-up of hydrogen sulphide, which would leave them no oxygen to breathe. Despite this problem and a few others these fertile regions of the Arabian Sea will prove to be among the world's most valuable fisheries. Probably the fertility period will last throughout the summer monsoon, from May to September. The density of the fish appears to be roughly comparable to that of the North Sea fishing areas.

In 1963 a great new source of fish food was located by the British Royal Research Ship *Discovery*, taking part in an international survey. Off the Arabian coast her scientists found that upwelling water brought to the surface large quantities of plankton and nutrient salt. At one point near the Kuria Muria islands the water was so heavy with plankton that the sea looked blood-red. The whole sea teemed with life—including possibly the biggest schools of dolphin yet seen.

The presence of such fishing grounds would make a marked difference to the health of people living around the Arabian Sea, for all lack protein in their diet. Karachi, Pakistan, where some of these people live, has one of the next interesting and ambitious fishing projects. The 'fish harbour project' takes the form of a complete and self-contained fishing community, the people of which build their own ships and gear and process and distribute their own fish. It is building up steadily with bigger ships, more distant waters and growing markets. One market is the United States, to which Karachi sells large deep-frozen prawns.

Good advice on fish-for-food has been given by Dr. George Humphrey, director of the Department of Fishing and Oceanography of the Australian National Research Council: 'There is enough fish in the world for everyone. But instead of expending their energy on snatching the fattest scraps away from one another, fishing nations should start examining the life and abode of the large shoals, and then think about how to distribute them.'

The Americans, through the Commercial Fisheries Bureau, are making steady progress in research. D. L. McKernan, director of the Bureau, had this to say: 'We can anticipate a vessel that would catch herring in the Pacific North-west, menhaden on the East Coast, threadfin herring in the Gulf of Mexico. The catch would be ground up, discharged into stainless steel tanks and treated with a mould or enzyme. While the vessel is at sea micro-organisms would digest the fish. When it reached port it would have a liquid mass in the hold. You could simply pump this out, spray-dry it and package it.' And it could be measured in thousands of tons.

The bureau is testing electric fields to increase the weight of a trawler's catch and claims that currents of varying voltage will sort out fish of different types and sizes. The bureau can already marshal fish or contain them in a given area by using a bubble screen through which the fish will not swim. The bureau predicts that within a few years fish will be sucked into very large trawlers through giant suction hoses, which would be much more efficient than nets.

Fisheries experts in several countries are now able to predict with fair accuracy in which direction and at what periods of the year certain fish will migrate, thus making it possible for trawlers to trap them.

However, it is a mistake to think that profitable fishing can occur anywhere. Most tropical waters do not have sufficient nutrients—plankton—to support abundant fish.

L   161

Bottom waters must be made to well up before fishing can become a commercial proposition in tropical waters. To this end the American National Academy of Sciences Committee on Oceanography plans to sink a nuclear reactor at a carefully selected spot in the sea to create vertical current circulation. This would force nutrients to the upper part of the sea to help support plankton, which attracts immense quantities of fish. The reactor would be placed in a normally unfruitful sea area. Another idea, well beyond the experimental stage, is to hang revolving blades in strong ocean currents; the currents would motivate the blades which would stir up the water, thus creating new fish pastures.

Despite the importance of open-sea or conventional fishing, fish-farming is possibly more important because it is under direct control and because it can be carried out in areas where food is urgently needed. It is much more developed than most people realize, but only in certain areas. Too much emphasis cannot be placed on fish-farming as a way of fighting the hunger problem, because it is something that can be done quickly and cheaply.

Thailand provides a revealing case history. A capable producer of food, mainly rice, Thailand has insufficient animal protein for its 34 million people. With great expanses of inland waters, she obviously had fish potential but, until 1951, she had small quantities of fish. In that year the Thai Government asked the F.A.O. to send a fishery specialist to the country to increase fish production. This expert's advice doubled the number of Thailand's ponds, tanks and output generally. The most impressive results came from a large swamp, which during the 'wet' supplied fish to 5,000 people. But in the dry season the swamp shrank alarmingly to a twentieth of its 'wet' size and great numbers of fish died.

The F.A.O. man organized the villagers into work teams. They improved swamp drainage, built mud walls, cleared out plants which choked the waters. They even agreed to fish according to regulations the expert proposed. He then

162

stocked the swamps with fast-growing and fast-breeding fish. Today that swamp produces about 120 per cent more fish than before—an annual catch of 110,000 kilograms. More than that, a purifying plant channels waters from the swamp to the houses of the villagers.

This Thai swamp was merely a pilot scheme. F.A.O. experts have helped to develop fish farming in Cambodia, Guatemala, India, Iraq, the Dominican Republic, Jordan, Honduras, Pakistan and Mexico. However, fish farming must become even more intensive and extensive.

Fish culture could turn to good use waterlogged and low land which might never be used for any other purpose, though ponds need to be carefully planned and regulated. In swampy areas unfit for any other form of food production fish-farming is the obvious thing.

Fish-farming can also be closely tied in to a general agricultural scheme. Cultivation of the water and the dry land around can form an organic whole in which animal droppings provide the main nutrients added to the fish ponds, and the water weeds grown in the ponds are used to feed the livestock.

It is common practice to combine fish-farming with rice growing, but millions more acres could be 'sown to fish'. Fish cultivation in rice fields is not only valuable in the quantity of fish produced, but can also increase the yields of rice.

One of the best fish for the purpose is the Tilapia Mosambica from East Africa, for it can thrive in salt water or brackish water, in still or running water, and being normally only the size of a pilchard, it can live in shallow water. The fish were introduced by chance to Java. A Dutch fish biologist happened to recognize five Tilapia found in a lagoon by a peasant and induced the Javanese people to cultivate them. The Thais developed the Tilapia 'project' by growing them to a bigger size in tanks in the middle of their rice fields. Now, by a curious twist, the Tilapia are being bred and nurtured

163

in Malawi, where they lived naturally in the first place.

Only in recent years has fish-farming been exploited as a crop for rural Africans, partly because the United Nations Special Fund paid for fish-farming to be developed at Kariba and at Lake Tanganyika. In Zambia there was a time when only Africans living near the main rivers and lakes ate fish, but as communications and catching methods improved larger quantities reached main centres. Zambia has eight large fish dams and 1,000 smaller ones scattered over the territory, and they produce about 1,000 tons a year; little, so far, compared with the 40,000 tons caught in natural waters. Cropping of many dams has been handicapped by tree stumps which were not cleared before the dams were flooded; but for the stumps the catch could be trebled.

The Fisheries Department stocks the various ponds with a total of about 125,000 live fish a year. The department advises Africans where and how to build a pond, which may be only a twentieth of an acre. About 20 lb. of fish are placed in a pond of a tenth of an acre and within a year this weight rises to about 120 lb., a very good dividend for the original investment. Fisheries officers visit the pond-owners to advise and help, with the result that they now have an all-year source of food and they crop during rains when market fish is scarce and prices high.

Demands for stock-fish come in frequently to the two departmental fish-farms at Chilanga and Mwekera. Mwekera has 40 ponds covering 16 acres and raises fish up to 3,000 lb. per acre per year. Important experiments made by the Zambian experts could well be used as a basis for any country or region planning to introduce or develop fish farming. For instance, it has been found that if an acre pond is stocked with 200 lb. of fish which are given no special food, the weight at the end of the year would be between 500 lb. and 800 lb. When fed with grass and vegetable waste the weight would increase to 1,000 lb., but by using mealie bran the weight can be brought up to as much as

3,000 lb. The Zambians have also found that ducks should be used on fish waters, for they fertilize it and help the growth of plankton. The cost is very low; some experiments show that fish can be raised for only $\frac{1}{2}$p a pound.

There are problems, of course. Ponds can only be fruitful where an assured year-round water supply is available—and for reasons of economy it must be natural water. In one day 5,000 gallons of water will evaporate from a pond covering a single acre and pumping water in to replace this loss would be costly. Water from a stream or spring is best. Poaching by otters, cormorants and by man can cause considerable losses: an otter will eat several pounds of fish a night and net-poachers can lift hundreds of pounds weight in an hour. Overstocking will defeat its own purpose for food then becomes scarcer and the fish are consequently smaller. And a pond must be competently built, then stocked with a suitable species of fish and given the correct food.

What has been done in Zambia could be done in many other regions if enough trained, dedicated workers and research and development stations were available. But even in Zambia one man is responsible for an area of 120,000 square miles. Less money should be spent on prestige works, such as huge dams, and more on fish farming which by itself could greatly increase the available food supply in areas that need it most. Big dams are important, but their benefits are often long term; people need to eat now.

The argument that fish-farming encourages disease-carrying mosquitoes is not valid, for many fish eat the larvae of mosquitoes as well as the water reeds on which the larvae grow. Fish are even more beneficial. They greatly help to control the crustaceans which carry the guinea-worm disease, and it is possible that over a period they could be an answer to the scourge of bilharzia. Bilharzia is spread by an infected freshwater snail which sheds many thousands of minute parasites. They normally live only about 72 hours unless they find a human host. The Zambia Fisheries Department has found that some species of bream eat snails, and they have been experimenting to find out which particular bream eat the bilharzia-carrying snails. It is believed that vast numbers of bream released into rivers like the Nile could check bilharzia and reduce it from a menace to a minor threat, not only in Egypt but in China and South America.

Most fish-farming is carried on in fresh or brackish waters and to only a limited extent in marine waters so far, but at a scientific conference in Geneva in February 1963 scientists seriously suggested that Pacific atolls should be enclosed and their lagoons made into fish and marine-life farms. These circular coral atolls of the South Seas would indeed provide ready-made fish ranches—or biatrons, as Jacques-Yves Cousteau called them.

Similarly, scientists advocate electric currents being passed across the mouths of fiords, rias and lochs. There is nothing dream-like about such a conception. Seafish-farming has already been tried in the British Isles—in Loch Sween, a Scottish inlet. Artificial fertilizers helped sea vegetation and natural fish food to grow prolifically and healthily, and consequently the fish themselves grew bigger. The fish migrated only because the loch water was colder than that of the open sea, but this could be overcome by warming the water; no insuperable task.

The F.A.O. believes that better use could be made of the wild stocks of fish in rivers, lakes and reservoirs of many countries. The undesirable species could be reduced and the waters stocked with better types. It is possible to improve water in several ways to support fish, and fish can also be protected against the dangers of chemical contamination. In true fish-farming strict control can be exercised over disease and parasitism.

Fish production can be increased by fertilizing areas with nitrogen and phosphates; the Russians are already doing this in bays and inlets. In Manila Bay fish and shrimp are being reared in fish-farms. Fed a mixture of soya flour, maize and barley, the fish are helping to fill the protein lack in the Philippines.

Not that artificial fertilizers are strictly necessary. The sea bottom is rich in natural fertilizers which could be brought back into use by some sort of pumping system.

Fish can be transplanted and controlled, and by the end of the century fishermen will catch fish where they want to do so and will not be forced to follow the fish. British scientists have been experimenting with young flounders since 1920, bringing them in containers to the rich waters around Britain. The Russians are introducing herring from northern waters to Antarctic regions which are relatively poor in fish life.

Diseases exist in marine plants and fish in certain regions, but several vast areas are virtually disease-free. One covers the region from Panama to Mexico, where yellowtails weigh as much as 100 lb. (they are a mere 20 lb. off California) and marlins weigh up to 2,500 lb. (normal weight about 250 lb.). For reasons like this much research is necessary before farming the sea for fish can become a major operation.

True fish are not the only living creatures that can be farmed. Several research projects are studying the possibility of farming the dolphin, the manatee and the dugong. The manatee especially has obvious advantages for farming. It is a large sea cow with a liking for shallow waters, including rivers and canals. In Guyana manatee are used to keep drainage ditches and canals clear of the fast-growing hyacinth weed. They could be used for the same purpose in hyacinth-choked rivers and lakes in many countries, including the Kariba Dam on the Zambesi.

The Japanese eat in quantity sea urchins, sea snails and sea slugs, all caught wild, while octopus and squid, bred in captivity and grown in sea-farms, are eaten cooked or raw. But perhaps eel takes first place in quantity. Japan has 800

167

eel farms, supplying, apart from thousands of shops, the 1,000 eel restaurants in Tokyo alone.

Shrimps and prawns have vast possibilities. A large mother prawn lays 1,250,000 eggs, but in the open sea only two or three live to be adult prawns. Under careful control this figure can be increased dramatically; one Japanese prawn farm produces nearly 2,000 tons annually.

Fish culture has reached such a successful stage in Japan that if the market is poor a fish farmer will sell some of his fish to fatteners who keep them in holding ponds until the price improves—in just the way that cattle and sheep are sold and fattened. The fish which take best to farming are bass, halibut, some kinds of mullet, breams and blowfish. Fish-farms are relatively cheap to establish, and very cheap to maintain. There is no physical reason why fish-farming could not become important in any country that desires to introduce it.

Fish flour is another marine product with tremendous possibilities. Already endorsed and encouraged by the F.A.O., it is simply fish reduced to liquid protein and dried to flour. It uses the whole fish, including the intestines, tail and head; ironically, the parts of the fish we throw away are the richest in vitamins. Other advantages are that fish flour is made cheaply, stored without refrigeration and is readily carried in bulk. The flour has many uses, from fish cakes to adding body to cereals, soups and bread. Fish flour is, after all, only a step forward from coarse fish meal, fed to fowls and animals. No cut in normal fish supplies would be necessary, for about 50 per cent of any catch is thrown overboard as useless and possibly 30 per cent is discarded in gutting and cleaning. The F.A.O. has supported a promotion campaign in Morocco.

The Japanese have also shown the lead in cultivation of marine vegetable life. They eat 20 kinds of seafood, more than anybody else. Some are harvested wild, others cultivated. Seaweed seed is planted in clam shells and later the seedlings are transplanted to nets. As it takes only two months to mature it provides a heavier yield per acre per year than any land crop. Seaweed is eaten with rice or fish, sprinkled on breakfast foods and biscuits, or as sticks. The Japanese know of 10,000 species of algae, sea plants and seaweeds eminently suitable for human food. Much of this food is already processed and marketed, often in cellophane bags, and it is as valuable in quality as any Western breakfast cereal. Certain species of seaweed have a protein content of 88 per cent or a fat content of 75 per cent of their total weight.

The Russians have caught on, and marine agronomists want to turn the Sea of Azov, part of the Black Sea and the Barents Sea into seaweed cultivation areas, with a growing depth of 300 feet.

In the not-too-distant future algae may form a bigger part of man's diet than fish. Given favourable conditions they multiply at an astonishing speed. In 1958, in Yellowstone National Park, U.S.A., a freshwater algae was discovered which reproduces 1,000 times in 24 hours. One of the few specialist algologists, Dr. C. M. Palmer, has stated that an ocean area the size of Rhode Island could produce enough algae to feed all the people on our planet, if cultivated properly. Simple facts would seem to bear out Dr. Palmer's claim. Algae can produce 50 crops in the time it takes wheat to produce one crop. An acre of land produces about a ton of wheat; an acre of algae could produce 50 tons. Algae are virtually 100 per cent usable, compared with the normal 5 to 10 per cent of a land plant.

Dr. W. J. Oswald has told the American Public Health Association that 5 million acres of algae-animal cultures could satisfy the entire protein needs of the U.S.A. although 300 million acres are now used in conventional agriculture.

Green algae, which grow in large quantities in all waters, can be raised in special cultures to give a startlingly high acre-yield. And as protein content can amount to 50 per cent of the total weight this is obviously a food to be exploited. Algae have even wider uses. They contain many chemical elements.

All this being so, why isn't more money and effort going into algae? The simple answer is apathy and conservatism.

Off the Norwegian coast brown kelp is being cultivated on a fairly large scale—about 200,000 tons a year. Much is used for animal feeding, but a lot is consumed by people. In Scandinavia and other Baltic countries much bread contains up to 10 per cent kelp meal; it gives the bread the taste of ordinary plain cake. Icelanders have been eating seaweed-meal bread since 1938.

In Illinois, Omaha, Kansas and other American states many farmers are using kelp meal for fodder and fertilizer. It contains 21 hormone and protein constituents and 64 other elements, including minerals, and is remarkably effective in strengthening undernourished animals and in making them disease-resistant. Within 20 years—some scientists say within 10 years—algin meal will become the chief animal fodder and it will be a prime fertilizer. When this happens a lot of land now used for pasture can be used for human-food crops.

Before long food chemists will succeed, for instance, in giving beef and pork flavour to seaweed, thus making it much more acceptable to the conservative and fastidious human palate. Modern advertising, which claims with some justice that it can sell anything, will have plenty of scope with seaweed and algae, but it will not be bending the truth when it claims that seaweed dishes are more nourishing than meat; this is simple fact

Aquaculture at depth—Jacques Cousteau called it 'thalasoculture'—has not yet started, but research indicates a vast potential of fish and other ocean food at depths of 1,000 feet. Here plankton, the basic food of all ocean life, seems to exist in the greatest quantity. Concentration of life is so intense that echo soundings detect a thick, moving layer—

170

clearly formed of living creatures—that lifts and falls to a daily rhythm. The layer could be enormous schools of fish, shrimp or squid. Whatever it is, it carries great promise for mankind, and it seems to me, as it seems to many people who have studied the problem, that salvation for mankind will come from the sea.

But a sober warning is necessary. We are dumping into the oceans vast quantities of pollutants—according to an estimate by the U.S. Food and Drug administration, no fewer than half a million substances.

Professor G. Cole, who has done much research on this problem, considers that 'We cannot assert that we are not poisoning the marine diatoms and thus bringing disaster upon ourselves.'* This poisoning can be seen, in concentrated form, in Lake Erie. In 1955 the lake supported commercial fishing, 75 million pounds of fish being taken. In 1967 Erie was a septic tank, a stinking mess in which there is no life at all, not even a snake. Lake Michigan has just about reached this stage; even Lake Baikal can be saved only with great effort and cost. Many of the world's rivers are approaching the stage of being too thin to plough and too thick to drink; the open sewer of the Rhine is a notable case.

Much of the world's population lives on or near coastlines and we tend to see estuaries and rivers in man-made roles: harbours, navigation channels, land-reclamation projects, sewage ponds, sand and gravel pits. This narrow vision triggers a tragic collision between human geography and natural geography. This is exemplified by San Francisco Bay which makes the city of San Francisco one of the most charming urban regions in the world. The bay traditionally serves as a vast marine nursery and a passageway for salmon and other fish. At one time, the Pacific coast's largest

* Address to the American Association for the Advancement of Science, December 27, 1967.

171

commercial fishing fleet docked in the bay. Today no commercial fishermen trawl their seine nets in its sunlit shallows.
The marine nursery exists largely as a giant cesspool, a garbage dump and a real estate reservoir.

As a cesspool, the bay receives the discharge of over 80
sewage outfalls. Daily, some 60 tons of greases and oils cas-
cade into the bay and paralyse the nerves of striped bass.
Acid wastes burn salmon gills and disrupt breathing. Paper-
mill effluents disrupt the normal division of eggs and fishermen catch freakish flounder. These wastes have transformed
the life-giving bay waters into a toxic broth.

Ninety per cent of the bay is closed to shellfish harvest.
Keeping it clear as a navigation channel means that fish
habitat is dredged up and oyster beds interred under slit
avalanches. As a garbage dump, marshes that once nurtured
eelgrass and other nutrients now exude only hot, pungent
odours of decay. Tideland habitat has been buried to accommodate apartments, shopping centres, airport runways
and athletic stadiums. A third of the bay—257 square miles
—has been reclaimed.

The bay that once annually provided 15 million lb. of
oysters, 300,000 lb. of clams and 7 million lb. of shrimps is
now sterile.

Such tragic waste is repeated in other estuary and river
systems throughout the world.

In the 1900's, fishermen on England's River Tees
harvested 8,000 lb. of salmon yearly; by the 1920's, 3,000 lb.;
now, virtually zero. A new and deadly tributary empties into
the Tees 12 million gallons of sewage daily. Sewage-nour-
ished 'blooms' of scum algae render some of Norway's deep
blue fjords opaque. These dense greenish blooms, by exhausting oxygen in the waters, suffocate marine life and
leave stinking windrows of dead fish on the beach.

The sea has great value in improving standards of living
generally, containing as it does so many minerals. In a single
cubic mile of sea water there is about 18 million tons of

magnesium chloride, 30 tons of copper, zinc and lead and up to 25 tons of gold.

Since over-population is inextricably bound up with food production, it might be as well for man to get busy on research into the idea of living on and under the sea, for there is no doubt that land living space will run out.

A Russian expert, Professor G. V. Petrovitch, urges that it would be cheaper to build cities on and below the seas than to build cities in space. Commander G. F. Bond of the U.S. Navy, an American expert in this new field says: 'The sea is the cheapest alternative for our overpopulated earth. . . . In a few hundred years there simply will not be room for man's ever-increasing numbers and agricultural lands will be too precious to erect new towns or factories on them.'

The Japanese are seriously planning to make the sea habitable. In Tokyo Bay by the end of the century there will be an undersea suburb with a diameter of 20 miles and a ceiling of 80 feet. Above the suburb will be its port, by which residents will travel to Tokyo itself. Tunnels under the sea will also connect the great suburb to the mainland. The Japanese are among the few peoples who appear to realize that long-range planning is necessary if the population explosion is to be beaten.

12 WORLD WATER SHORTAGE; SALINITY; IRRIGATION

The world is running short of fresh water. This is the sober truth and some governments, including those of the United States and Britain, are acutely conscious of it. Shortage of fresh water is almost as serious as the shortage of food, and the world's people should be under no illusions about it, even though the entire human race swallows less than one-hundred-thousandth of the annual rainfall on land each year.

Professor J. R. A. McMillan, Dean of the Faculty of Agriculture at Sydney University, warned in September 1965 that because of the serious shortage of water man would become largely vegetarian in order to survive. Speaking to the Association for the Advancement of Science, he said that at the present rate of consumption world water resources could not support a population of more that 2,500 million. The world will have three times this number by A.D. 2000.

Professor McMillan makes the point that the raising of animals to provide meat is one of the most wasteful forms of food production in terms of water usage. Since it takes 50 tons of water to produce one pound of meat and as 80 per cent of Australia's rainfall is required for the country's present meat consumption, his argument is valid as it concerns Australia, though the position is hardly so crucial in, say, Britain. However, Professor McMillan says bluntly that man will be forced increasingly to replace meat with vegetable proteins readily available from leaves.

'The real problem,' he stresses, 'is getting enough water for food production. No time must be lost in planning the conservation of the world's water resources.'

The need for water conservation, even in areas of regular rainfall such as Britain, is not fully appreciated. Industry has an insatiable appetite; 45,000 gallons of water are needed to make one motor car, 120,000 gallons to make one ton of aluminium, 240,000 gallons to make a ton of newsprint. Experiments in Australia have shown that to grow the grain for a single loaf of bread two and a half tons of water are needed and that one ton is needed for a fowl to lay one egg.

It may not be long before Britain and other countries need a national water grid so that drier areas can import water from wetter ones. This would be fraught with dangers. Dr. R. L. Nace, research hydrologist with the U.S. Geological Survey, says that projects which reverse the flow of great river systems, could slow the earth's rotation and increase the degree to which it wobbles on its axis.* He was referring specifically to schemes in North America and the Soviet Union to send rivers flowing south to supply thirsty populous areas instead of allowing them to follow their natural course northward through empty waste. Nace also sees another effect—a change in the heat balance of the regions affected. 'We don't even know what is happening in nature,' he said, 'We cannot predict what will happen under man's influence.'

* An address to an international conference, Paris, 1969, on the progress of the International Hydrological Decade.

The amount of water vapour the atmosphere can hold depends on its temperature. Rain is caused by moist air cooling below the point where it can no longer hold all its water in vapour form. The motivating force for the water cycle—evaporation, condensation and back to water again —is the sun, which sucks up the moisture from soil, vegetation and sea. Over the world the annual volume of water evaporated and precipitated amounts to nearly 100,000 cubic miles, which happens to be sufficient to submerge the globe under 31 inches of water. But of this tremendous amount about 85 per cent is fed back to the oceans; only a quarter, 24,000 cubic miles, falls on the land and two-fifths of this finds its way back to the sea. This means that the world's useful rainfall is only five inches a year.

To put the situation another way, at present most of the earth's rainwater flows into the sea as rivers, or is evaporated. Rivers account for 9,000 million gallons annually. Only about $3\frac{1}{2}$ per cent of this river flow is diverted for irrigation and it is spread over only 1 per cent of the earth's land. The remaining 99 per cent of cultivated but unirrigated land uses another 3,000 million gallons a year—a fraction of what is potentially available.

The almost universal drought of 1965, the worst in recorded history, was a warning of what will happen if the world does not act now to conserve water and to find means of 'making' it.

The drought in the north-eastern states of the U.S.A., from Maine to northern Virginia and including the Appalachians, had started in 1961. At one time New York's complex water storage system was officially at an 'acutely dangerous level'. The city's 320 fountains were turned off and restaurants were fined if they put water on tables, unless it happened to be ordered. Inevitably New York must become even more chronically short of water and some experts see it as a 'parched city'.

In 1965, too, much of southern Africa, from the Limpopo

veldt to the usually green hills of Eastern Cape Province had the worst drought in memory. It had then lasted three years and many white farmers faced ruin and bankruptcy while natives faced their traditional enemies—hunger and misery. Spain, Portugal, northern Italy and southern France were seriously affected. Spain lost most of her wheat crop and Portugal's water supply sank to such a low ebb that she had to import hydro-electric power. Italy's rice crop was also seriously damaged.

In Southern America, Uruguay suffered from the same scourge, losing many cattle, while Mexico lost much of her cotton crop. A long drought through eastern Australia forced farmers to sell sheep at a shilling a head merely to gain some return for them. Drought in China caused another poor harvest for rice and wheat, and in South Korea rice was hit by the worst drought in 10 years.

The drought brought vivid emphasis to the need for universal water conservation and storage and for further research into possible areas of underground water still waiting to be tapped. Hydrologists now realize that possibly nine-tenths of the world's fresh water is not on the ground, but under it. Vast amounts lie under desert countries such as Libya, Algeria, Tunisia, Mauretania and Egypt, as well as parts of the Gobi Desert.

Yet according to W.H.O. surveys, over nine-tenths of the people of the developing world do not have enough water and the quality of what they do obtain is generally poor. W.H.O. estimates that 500 million people are infected by water-borne disease.

With increasing urbanization and industrialization and the inevitable increase in water consumption and with more and more water needed for irrigation, rainfall cannot be depended upon. Since 1961 the rain pattern has been steadily changing, with less in the middle and high latitudes and more in the tropics. Concurrently, the historically reliable rain-bearing westerlies in the middle latitudes have been

M   177

blowing less frequently and less strongly. I cannot be concerned here with possible scientific explanations. What matters is that short-term and long-term steps must be taken to prepare for the inevitable water shortage.

The total basic water supply available in the United States, for instance, is about 515,000 million gallons a day; Americans are already using 375,000 million gallons of it. The margin is insufficient, for in the past 20 years America has doubled her water consumption and by 1985 will probably double it again. Obviously, many regions face critical water shortages. The situation confronts most industrial countries to a greater or lesser degree.

Paul Ehrlich says that if the current rape of American watersheds and the population and water use trends continue, in 1984 the United States will be 'quite literally' dying of thirst.*

Athelstan Spilhaus believes that the ultimate situation to the population problem for a closed-system earth is to use, re-use and recycle wastes. For instance, water could be used first for drinking and then re-used at least twice, for cooling and then for recreation.

The United States is spending much money on research into purifying seawater. Industry and agriculture consume vast quantities of water. Even in Britain, where people often complain about the rain, there is threat of a water shortage and a few hot weeks in summer without any rain brings on talk of 'emergency measures'. Emergency measures are in use in some areas, such as outback Australia, and many countries have to hoard water as one of their most precious commodities. If all the rainfall were spread evenly over the globe there would be plenty for every foreseeable purpose. But rainfall distribution, like that of food, is very uneven—both in space and time—and the world is only just beginning to look after it properly. Not that even the most extreme care will make any difference to the Sahara, the Kalahari,

* The Population Bomb.

the Gobi and Central Asian deserts, the Australian interior, parts of the western U.S.A. and the Antarctic. Short of really revolutionary schemes, these huge parched areas will remain parched, just as most of the lands adjoining them will remain arid.

There is much speculative talk of changing desert climates. One scheme is to coat about 25 square miles of North African desert with bitumen which will reflect great heat, cause convection currents to rise which in theory would condense and form clouds, and then drop rain.

The principle works naturally with burning oil wells and forest fires, both of which often generate thunderstorms. The same principle is at work in the great French meteotron on the Lannemezan plateau in the central Pyrenees. One hundred great oil-fired burners around an area of 3,200 square metres can produce up to 700,000 kilowatts of power, a thermal capacity great enough to upset nature's balance. Under ideal conditions, the plant can produce its first artificial cumulus cloud in six minutes. The French scheme, largely experimental, has influenced other countries to build super meteotrons. In some regions a large meteotron could increase rain over an area of 500 square miles by as much as 30 per cent. This would make a radical difference to areas of outback Australia, for instance.

Another scheme, already planned, is to fill up the Qattara Depression, North Africa, with Mediterranean water via a canal. The large lake resulting from this, would, it is believed, change the climate of the surrounding regions. There are even schemes to control the weather. But if a great climatic change could be caused in one area it could easily upset the delicate balance of the weather and produce a new desert elsewhere.

One of the most interesting and cheapest ideas is to use the heat of the sun to distil water, especially as several deserts are close to the sea and so combine plenty of sun with vast amounts of seawater. The main problem is cost. The sun does not give concentrated heat and very large areas are needed to collect the solar energy. The cost of such an installation is high to the amount of water produced, and it would be economically impracticable to use water so gained for crop irrigation.

The world already has about 100 de-salting plants producing a total of 1,000 million gallons a day, with many more under construction. The American company, Westinghouse, has built four distillation plants for water-starved Kuwait; the plants now purify Persian Gulf water at the rate of 5,200,000 gallons a day. Other big distillation plants are operating in Egypt, Libya, Saudi Arabia, Indonesia, Malta and the Virgin Islands. The largest seawater conversion unit in the U.S. is at Freeport, Texas, which produces 1,200,000 gallons a day. The United States government is well aware of the impending shortage of fresh water and is spending millions of dollars a year on research and plant.

One project stands out among the plans for the future. On an artificial island, a mile off the Californian coast, the Americans are building the world's largest atom-powered water-works. It has two nuclear reactors with a joint output of 1,800 megawatts and can supply a city of 2,000,000 with electricity and 750,000 people with drinking water from the sea. From 1972, it will be able to convert 200 million litres of sea water economically into drinking water every day and, eventually, 600 million litres daily.

From a global and food point of view the developing techniques of water purification are significant. The world has many islands at present supporting no population or a relatively small one because of lack of water, needed not only for domestic use but for crops and stock. Already a major pilot scheme has shown that provided a certain amount of solar heat exists fresh water can be won at a low cost. The scheme was that which brought water to the island of Symi, one of the many Greek Aegean islands which have very low rainfall. The world's first full-scale plastic solar still makes fresh water from the sea at a rate of 5,000 gallons a day, an adequate amount for the 3,000 inhabitants.

The scheme is based on a system of narrow ponds about 250 feet long lined with rubber and black material to absorb the sun's rays. Each pond is covered with a transparent plastic tent. Sea water is pumped into the ponds at night, then during the day the sun evaporates the water, which condenses on the plastic and runs into a reservoir. The water costs about 88p per 1,000 gallons compared with £3·15 for the same amount before introduction of the scheme. Most Greek islands, with their assured sunshine, will eventually have solar stills, with a resulting increase in food production and standard of living. Similiar schemes on a larger scale could be used to develop, for example, the semi-desert of the California peninsula, the desert valleys of the Rockies and the south-western states of the United States, the desert coastlands of southern and western Australia, south-west and north-west Africa, northern Chile, and many now-unpopulated islands.

The solar still system will work efficiently only where sunshine is frequent and long, as in the places mentioned. Where this is not the case sea water can be heated and sprayed into a low-pressure chamber, where a part of it boils into vapour and evaporates into fresh water. It is also possible to freeze sea water and extract the fresh water from it. In this system cooling gas is piped into a reservoir of sea water. As the gas evaporates it chills the water and causes ice crystals to form without salt. When washed and melted the crystals provide large amounts of fresh water at less cost than the boiling system. The industrial east of the U.S.A., northern Italy, Britain and Belgium are among the countries which may well be forced to find fresh water by these methods.

Really big nuclear power plants—on the California model could do much for the eastern and southern Mediterranean from Israel to Morocco. This area could become as prosperous as when much of it was the Roman empire, with a vastly increased production of vegetables and fruit. It is barely possible to speak of water or food without speaking of the other, and in the years to come they must be integrated in all planning.

Gibraltar is an obvious place for many experiments in water production. One particular experiment, little publicized, could bring water to certain areas. The basic requirements are land at a height of about 1,000 feet in the path of a strong wind, blowing from the sea. At this height in Gibraltar two screens of fine wire mesh, each about three feet by six feet, were set up in the path of the frequent strong winds. Each square foot of mesh yielded a minimum of seven gallons of water during summer—the dry half of the year— and five gallons during the winter, with an additional eight gallons from rain during the winter. In practical pay-off terms, 10,000 square feet of mesh would win a quarter of a million gallons of fresh water annually, a valuable contribution to a chronically water-short place like Gibraltar. This is one of the cheapest ways of getting water, for after the initial outlay the only cost is maintenance of the mesh. The catch is better in summer because easterly winds are then blowing over a large part of the warm Mediterranean, thus absorbing more moisture than the westerlies which blow from the colder Atlantic.

But water has its drawbacks and can cause as much trouble as a plague of locusts. The Indus in West Pakistan carries twice as much water as the Nile and half of it is diverted into irrigation canals, so that today the Indus plain is the largest irrigated area in the world and supports 30 million people. But poor drainage, waterlogging and salinity are gradually destroying fertility and more than 100,000 acres are being lost to cultivation each year; a loss that neither Pakistan nor the world can afford.

The great Indus valley is very flat, and deep in alluvium and perhaps also in some loess. Groundwater has always been present in this soil, and while it was a certain depth it caused no anxiety, but in places it has risen alarmingly or is rising now, so that land is constantly going out of production. Some is reclaimed, but the situation worsens steadily.

The immensity of the Indus irrigation scheme makes this Pakistan's most serious problem. One of seven canals beginning at the great Sukkur barrage is several times larger than the Thames. It is the Rohri Canal, more than 200 miles long, irrigating 2 million acres with its 10,000 cubic feet of water a second. Unfortunately the region has no natural drainage, so that water, percolating through the soil in many ways, gradually built up the water table. The danger was recognized by experts about 1922, but since the problem was then only a projected one, neither government nor farmers would spare money or time on it. Drainage in several forms now carry away some of the excess water, but the situation is still critical and it has ruined thousands of poor farmers.

Control of salt is extremely difficult. Salt can be dissolved and carried deep into the soil by fresh water poured on to the land, but evaporation at the surface frequently draws the salt up again, back to the soil's root-zone, thus damaging or destroying crops. An aerial photograph shows great whitened areas of salted land. The areas are so large and the cost so immense that no government could provide free drainage; the farmers cannot help financially unless they can increase productivity, and this they cannot do while much of their land is useless.

Schemes to resurrect the plains have been worked out— largely by two British firms—but getting them to work is more difficult. Sheer ignorance and hunger-apathy often prevents farmers from co-operating. Nevertheless work is in progress to drain 29 million acres; this involves the building of 31,500 tube wells, 7,500 miles of major drainage canals and 25,000 miles of supplementary drains. The Central

Rechna Doab was the first area to be treated. Pumps attached to the tube wells have reduced the water table as much as seven feet. The water gained is spread over the land again in large quantities to wash the salts out of surface layers while drains carry away the surplus. In Rechna Doab food production is expected to increase by 500,000 tons.

Apart from its intrinsic value, water, used in irrigation, is one of the major methods by which food production can be stepped up. Irrigation, indeed, receives more attention and is the subject of more schemes than any other aspect of food production. This is encouraging, but only about 300 millions acres are under irrigation throughout the world, and liaison and international exchange of knowledge about irrigation is practically nil. Some schemes have been in existence for many years without achieving much publicity, although modifications of them could be adopted in other areas.

It is difficult to give an accurate figure of the number of people wholly dependent on irrigation for their livelihood and indirectly dependent on it for at least part of their food supplies. However, conservative estimates would be 200 million and 600 million. Some countries, notably West Pakistan, Iraq and Egypt would find survival difficult without irrigation.

There is nothing new about the principle of irrigation, except the engineering methods used to apply it and many of the most modern ones are based on ancient techniques. But today's schemes are vast, complex and ambitious. Vast, like that of the Indus Basin; complex, like many in the U.S.A.; and ambitious, like the Snowy River scheme in East Australia; and all three, like those in Russia. Nearly all the big irrigation schemes have been developed since 1900 and many of them since 1945.

There is a natural tendency to associate irrigation only with extreme aridity, yet many places which are irrigated have a reasonable annual rainfall. The total annual rainfall in parts of Italy is not necessarily less than that of south-east England, but it is not so evenly distributed. Another misconception about irrigation is that it is used only to water human food crops. This was certainly so until recent times, but modern irrigation also waters stock pastures. As this increases the available meat supply it is an important aspect of food production. Pasture irrigation is practised in a rela-tively large way in the United States, mainly on parts of the High Plains and in southern Texas. It is under experi-ment in Australia, the Transvaal, the southern Soviet Union, southern France and Mexico.

Irrigation is necessary wherever rainfall is inadequate, according to the simple yardstick of insufficient inches per year, or where it is unevenly distributed, according to the more complicated seasonal requirements of crops.

Much has been done or is in progress, but much remains to be done. A major irrigation project takes years from its conception to the time it produces food. Irrigation is ade-quate probably in only three countries to keep pace with the increasing food requirements of the population—the United States, the Soviet Union and Australia. Only a few countries can claim to need no irrigation for the time being —New Zealand and Eire are good examples. Even Norway, Sweden and Finland practise irrigation.

It would be wrong to suppose that all water-short areas could be irrigated. It is also wrong to talk glibly of 'irrigat-ing the deserts'. A realistic approach is necessary. 'The very deserts can be made fertile,' says one writer enthusiastically, and for his example points to the craze for desert-living in California. True desert cannot be made fertile enough to pro-duce crops, no matter what is done to it.* The few people who live in basically arid country in California are not at the same time living *from* it. That they manage to have gar-dens is a tribute to their own wealth—they often have many

* Many deserts were *once* fertile. Three thousand years B.C. the Sahara was green with crops and trees.

tons of good soil brought from elsewhere—and to their landscape gardener's ingenuity. The people who live in parts of the Sahara have neither wealth nor landscape gardeners.

No irrigation engineer would contemplate irrigating a desert if he could find more suitable land to irrigate, and successful irrigation of a true desert—e.g. Simpson's Desert in Australia or the Libyan Desert—would present enormous problems. It is not enough to bring water to the desert, for the soil is so thin that moisture drains away or is evaporated by the hot sun. The lands must be given body by careful planting of trees and shrubs with thick roots that can store water.

Relatively small areas are true deserts, but in only four countries has serious research begun to develop the semi-desert and arid lands—Australia, Egypt, Israel and Russia.

Australia's great Snowy River scheme which, in essence, called for reversing the flow of a river so that it would flow inland instead of to the sea, showed that this is one country which is thinking big. The need for more food demands that nations think big. Australia may well have to think so very big as to undertake to bring water from the mountains of New Guinea to the arid central plains of the mainland, as I hinted in an earlier chapter. The idea, not before suggested, is feasible but would be expensive. Tropical rain falls heavily every day in the highlands of Papua and New Guinea; the water could be easily caught and stored but getting it to Australia via pipeline would be a major engineering task. Still, it would be a task in which Australia has had experience. There is already a water line running from the coast of Western Australia to the goldfield towns, 300 miles away. In the Eyre Peninsula of South Australia irrigation water is taken 250 miles by pipe and tapped along the way. The Whyalla scheme, a similar one, depends on water piped from the Murray River. South Australia alone has 8,300 miles of irrigation water pipes.

Another big scheme—piped water from the Andes or

perhaps from the Amazon River—could bring food to starving areas of Brazil.

Fortunately, there is now a universal acceptance of the need for irrigation. Even peasant farmers who resist the use of animal manure on their land can see the benefit of irrigation. They will have nothing to do with scientific means of farming or artificial fertilizers, but they will accept artificial watering.

But irrigation is not a uniform science. A successful scheme in Spain would not necessarily be successful in Australia. Soil, slope, rate of evaporation, amount of rainfall, drainage, type of crops grown—all these factors must be considered before a modern irrigation project can be commenced.

The huerta of south-east Spain—an area of Murcia producing vegetables and fruit—is a prime example of what can be accomplished in an area of low rainfall. Every inch of this huerta is carefully cultivated with an almost unbelievable variety of products—corn, pepper, olives, rice, table vegetables such as parsley, egg-plant, beans, almonds, dates, oranges, figs, pears, peaches, apricots, apples, quinces, lemons, grapefruit, pomegranates. In addition 45,000 acres are under cotton and a large area is covered by mulberry trees on which silk worms spin their cocoons. Yet the average annual rainfall is a mere 10 inches, the summer temperatures soar to 114 degrees and rivers dry up. In spring and autumn floods rage down the watercourses.

The agricultural prosperity of the Murcia huerta—as with other Spanish huertas—is due to a complex and efficient system of irrigation begun by the Romans, fostered by the Visigoths and brought to perfection by the Arabs. Because water is scarce it is carefully distributed, usually by methods dating back to Moorish occupation. Methods differ from area to area, but generally each farmer is allowed a period of time to release water from the main canal into his own channels. Some underground water is obtained, usually by

187

a blindfolded mule which plods round and round turning the wheels that raise the water containers.

Much of the fruit is canned locally—in tin imported in pieces from Britain and assembled by local women—and then exported to Britain and elsewhere. The whole area is practically self-contained and its prosperity is assured.

Allied to this 1,000-year-old system are new and more expensive water storage techniques, including underground reservoirs where water, trapped during the occasionally heavy deluges, is safe from evaporation in the hot sun.

The methods of trapping and storing the water for irrigation could be used in other Mediterranean countries, in California, in several parts of Australia and in many islands suffering from recurring water shortages, such as Hong Kong. Improvements in the Jordan Valley scheme, which loses several million tons of water daily through evaporation in summer, are similar to those incorporated in the Spanish system.

Just as Russia has taken the lead in oceanography, so is she in first place with irrigation, though considering her vast area this is not surprising. Uzbekistan, the first part of the Soviet Union to undertake large scale irrigation, has brought into use more than 2 million acres. Seventy districts of Azerbaijan state have been developed by irrigation, with canals of 28,000 miles. The main area is that of the Kura-Aras lowlands; canals have been built from the Kura and the Aras to the Karabakh, Shirvan, Mil and Salian steppes. The scheme is one of the most intensive in the world and is responsible for a vast agricultural output. In Armenia about 700,000 acres are under irrigation, the main scheme being on the Kotaiski plan. Vast orchards and vineyards have been laid out in what were semi-desert areas, now watered by the Talin, Arzni-Shamiram and Kotaiski Canals. The yield of some crops is expected to rise by 300 per cent and fruit by 500 per cent. About 90 per cent of Turkmenia is occupied by the Karakum Desert, but slices of it are being reclaimed by projects taking the waters of the Amu-Darya across the desert. The big irrigation schemes of the Sumbar and Atrek valleys in the extreme south-west grow dates and olives, pomegranates, citrus and other fruits. Turkmenian irrigation is probably the best example of an old system modernized. It was completely rebuilt in 10 years. Small systems were joined into big ones, waste was eliminated, locks were built to control flow from head reservoirs, gravity-flow canals replaced water wheels. The Karakum Canal, one of the biggest irrigation projects existing, was built under difficult conditions which illustrate what irrigation engineers can do. The canal is 560 miles long and will irrigate a million acres.

It is not possible here to go into details about the many irrigation schemes in progress, and it would be misleading to suggest that irrigation could work miracles. Less than 10 per cent of present world food production comes from irrigated or artificially drained land and less than 5 per cent of this total depends on control of water on an engineering scale. Herbert Addison, an irrigation expert with 30 years' experience in the Middle East, believes that of the estimated increase in world food production during the half century to 2,000 not more than a tenth of the total can be expected as a result of new large-scale engineering works.

But I see much hope in this sober estimation, because, considering how large the population will be by the end of the century a tenth of the total food requirements is a large proportion. In any case, I believe that man will be collectively intelligent enough to add continuously to irrigation works, so that the proportion of food produced on them will continue to grow.

Dr. Ehrman is flatly pessimistic about irrigation as a major weapon in the food fight. He says, in effect, 'We cannot expect great increases in food through placing more land under cultivation. With rare exceptions land that is not already farmed is not farmed for sound reasons—poor soil, lack of water, unsuitable climate. Some areas *could* be farmed—at enormous cost in money, energy and effort. Even given all these, it is unlikely that farming of the fringe areas could mitigate the coming crisis.'

However, many of the interesting irrigation projects in various parts of the world provide some hope for humanity. Irrigation, though an ancient science—it was first practised 7,000 years ago in Asia Minor—has captured the imagination of governments since 1945 and it is the one thing connected with food production that has moved at anything like an adequate rate.

On an international scale of values land-reclamation in the form of polders is a very unimportant contribution to food production. Polders have certainly helped the Dutch economy, but they cost a tremendous amount of time and money and they make up a small part of the total farming area. Schemes to reclaim vast areas of sea are harebrained and financially prohibitive. Very few areas would be suitable for poldering; the Dutch Zuider Zee (now Ijssel Meer) happened to be peculiarly suitable for the operation.

However, reclaiming of swampland does have possibilities, as shown in India. In 1950 about one and a half million acres in the Himalaya Terai of India were malarial jungle swamp with 75 per cent of people in the area suffering from malaria. Seven years later, after a lot of hard work by F.A.O. and W.H.O. experts, malaria had disappeared and a tenth of the swamp was fertile soil under cultivation. In time virtually all the swamp will disappear. Almost every country in the world has areas of swamp and marsh which could become useful farming country, and as they constitute short-term or medium-term projects they could be producing food in time for the super-crisis hunger period.

13 TREES AND SOIL EROSION

By cutting down trees to establish farms our ancestors ensured that we would have food and agricultural headaches
today. According to J. H. Scott Watson, in the *Agricultural
Institute Review*, an average of 13 million acres are being
lost to the world every year through erosion. This means
that every day 36,000 acres disappear, an appalling loss as
population increases. And largely because people of former
times cut down trees. About half the original fertile land
of the earth has been lost since people formed themselves
into states a few thousand years ago and thus made demands
for food on the surrounding countryside.

The life of man, in the form of the food, air and water
which sustain and nourish him, is bound up with forest and
the natural cycle of which it is part. The great catastrophes
of the Mississippi floods, the Dust Bowl of the Middle West,
the famines of China, the terrifying Australian droughts,
the creeping spread of the deserts—all these have resulted
from destruction of forest cover.

191

The world's people, as a whole, are lamentably ignorant about the relationship of trees to food problems and few disciples have arisen to teach them. Richard St. Barbe Baker spent most of his life in the work and made impassioned pleas to man not to destroy himself by destroying trees, but he did not make the impression he deserved.

Trees are possibly Nature's most efficient means of soil defence, as soil conservation exponents have found while using them 'artificially'. They tie down steep hillsides, check the growth of gullies, steady stream banks which might otherwise collapse, and screen cultivated fields from damaging winds. Cut judiciously they add to a farm's income, for they provide fuel, fence posts, timber for buildings and a marketable produce.

History has enough lessons about the penalty of destruction. The empires of Babylon, Syria, Persia and Carthage were destroyed by the advance of floods and deserts caused by the increasing clearing of forests for farmland. Each year for centuries the Yellow River of China has washed away 2,500,000 tons of useful soil. A complex and ambitious scheme to check this wastage is in progress, and though many centuries late, is not too late to improve food production greatly through better land use and water conservation.

Apart from all this, every farm has land that will not produce crops but virtually no land so poor that it cannot produce trees. And trees, in one way or another, add to income and thus increase standards of living.

The health and economic security of man is firmly bound with efficient forest and tree management. The forest is 'the mother of the rivers', as has been so poetically expressed, for it is an important natural means of maintaining and regulating water flow. The state of forests decides whether rain and snow will be beneficial or catastrophic. When vast areas of forest are removed the whole water pattern changes, leading to profound differences in agriculture and stock raising. Also, urban water-users and valley,

192

dwellers, remote though they may be from a watershed, are influenced by what happens in forest uplands. Meddling with the natural circulation of water is criminal negligence, if only because it results in the loss of incalculably vast amounts of soil.

Forest areas help to equalize temperature, to precipitate clouds and increase rainfall. Trees usually increase horizontal precipitation while their leaves retain the moisture, stopping a quick run-off to the ground below. Time is needed for rain to permeate the leaves, and more time is needed for the water to penetrate the humus. More time is taken by the water finding its way through the root channels to the subsoil, where in due course it will form springs that foster rivers. All the vegetation retards evaporation. The whole result is that the water level is kept high but under control; thus forests provide the best catchment areas.

Trees, too, are completely self-supporting; they need no fertilizers; they supply their own through the yearly fall of leaves, twigs and bark.

Too many farmers in many parts of the world, ignorant through no fault of their own, cut down all their trees in the belief that the more ground they can cultivate the better. It seems to me, from travels in many countries, that governments are doing little to restore the situation, which, already serious, could reach critical proportions. However, the F.A.O. is alert to the danger.

Perhaps paradoxically, North America has been the most remarkable arena in which Man has seemed bent on destroying himself. The early settlers cleared large areas of forest, found the soil rich and grew heavy wheat crops year after year. When a farm showed signs of exhaustion some settlers moved on. Many farmers almost literally saw the soil vanish from under their feet—at a rate of about an inch in depth a year. The sheer tragedy of this can be realized when measured against the time taken to build up an inch of soil—400 years.

N
193

Crops thinned the soil and heat, rain and wind began to carry it away, whole farmloads at a time. Rain cut gullies in the soil or washed it away in sheets, and finally erosion generally left 1,000 million acres either ruined or badly damaged. Before they realized the danger, the Americans had cut seven-eighths of their virgin forests and were left with only 284,000 square miles of exploitable forest.

Not until the 1930s did soil conservation become a matter of national urgency in the U.S.A., but then, with typical American drive and thoroughness, the war against soil loss has been complex and largely effective. The soil and land already lost can be reclaimed in only a few cases, but the wastage has been stopped, despite the insatiable demands for paper in a country in which one edition of a single Sunday newspaper consumes 23 acres of trees.

In the Tennessee Valley of the eastern U.S.A. straight lines of trees hold together land that was once uninhabitable because of erosion. Schemes such as the Tennessee Valley one, with its reafforestation, river control, water conservation and planned agriculture costs much more money than most nations can afford.

The difference trees can make has never been better proved than by J. J. Lydick of Craig, Nebraska. About 1918 he started planting rows of shelter trees on his 240-acre farm, which was in a treeless area only two miles from an area of windblown soil—loess. Average annual precipitation was 28 inches, but some years this fell to 15. In this arid, windy and dusty area the water table was at 60 feet.

Lydick raised pines, spruce, poplar and fir in nursery beds and planted slower-growing trees on the outside and evergreens inside. They became a thick—up to 60 feet across—impenetrable barrier against winds and storms, and Lydick gave his trees priority with his time, despite the ridicule of other farmers. Droughts hit Nebraska in 1934 and 1936, but not a single conifer was lost. Lydick's acres yielded twice as much as those owned by other farmers. In 1934 he

dug 200 bushels of potatoes to the acre, though other farmers for a 10-mile radius around his property found none
to dig. Lydick had no irrigation, but he harvested about 40
bushels of corn to the acre, while neighbours were virtually
without crops owing to hot winds that summer. Lydick's
orchards flourished—with heavy yields of apples and rasp-
berries. His success caused so much interest that he was
frequently asked to account for it. It was, he said, a matter
of common sense. In winter his trees trapped snow, which
melted on the spot, instead of being piled into drifts some
distance away. In summer the trees took the speed out of
drying winds, thus little moisture was lost from the soil.
Also, he lost no soil to these winds; for his trees prevented
erosion. When other farmers' soils were being desiccated
Lydick's were light, friable and moist because of the trees'
influence.

Iraq furnishes another type of example. Here agricultural
expansion has driven nomadic herdsmen into grazing their
stock in forest lands. This practice, as uncontrolled as it is
destructive, has led to the disappearance of tree cover needed
to protect agricultural land and crops and their regular supply of water. Directly, it has deprived the country of a raw
material which yearly becomes more important for houses,
furniture, paper and books, textiles and many other things.

Iraq's pressing problems would be eased if she devoted
more land to timber in agricultural regions. She would not
then have to spend so much money on imports of timber
and pulp. Trees would provide additional income for
farmers already straining to make a living; they would
provide off-season employment in many ways, including, for
instance, the making of boxes. Trees, too, can be an important source of fodder for livestock; the organ tree, for example. Cows feed on its fruit, goats and camels eat its leaves.
It also provides valuable oil. Where soil is thin and less
fertile trees will grow where other crops will not. More than
four-fifths of Iraq is desert or steppe and rainfall is poor,

but crops could be improved if trees were more closely allied to agriculture. From a practical point of view revenue from tree crops compares adequately with that from cash crops, especially in arid countries.

Trees are very necessary in many areas, for they form windbreaks against not only wind itself but against sand and dust storms. They lessen the damage caused by drying winds. More intense local tree cover has an influence on climate by reducing extremes of temperature, increasing atmospheric humidity and lowering evaporation rates. More than this, tree cover is the best way of controlling erosion. The F.A.O. believes that tree planting is the solution to many of Iraq's problems and its experts introduced the best and most suitable strains of poplar and eucalyptus. Demonstration areas in Iraq are open to farmers, and many have availed themselves of the F.A.O.'s advice and practical help. Even with the quick-growing trees recommended by the F.A.O. it will still be 10 years before the benefits of tree growing will make themselves felt. But at least the F.A.O. realizes that much must be done *now*, that this is a matter of top priority.

World afforestation could not only check and stop the advance of deserts, but in time could reverse the trend. Ghana, then the Gold Coast, suffered terribly from destruction of trees along its border with the desert, and in the 1940's this had reached such serious proportions that chiefs forbade marriage and women refused to have children because they knew they could only die of hunger.

Israel is another country that would benefit from a vast tree-planting programme. Its whole area could be reafforested at relatively little cost and, in fact, many nurseries are flourishing and the Negev desert now has large patches of tree cover.

Britain has her own problem, for much of the country consists of steep hillsides which urgently need forest covering if they are to be reclaimed. The minimum of safety in tree cover is, from all points of view, a tenth of the habitable land area. Britain's total forest covering is less than a sixteenth of which, incidentally, only half is of any economic value.

Reafforestation is the major part of any scheme to fight erosion, but there are other aspects, such as contour ploughing and planting, care in soil use so that it does not become so thin that it will lift with a wind, and filling in of ravines and gullies so that they will not continue to widen. The world cannot afford to lose more soil, and the spectacle of some men working industriously and expensively to reclaim certain areas while other men let their areas go to ruin is ridiculous.

Forests need much research, especially tropical forests which contain such a vast variety of trees, thus making commercial exploitation difficult and unprofitable. Yet the tropics have the advantage of remarkably rapid growth in trees: a conifer that needs up to 100 years to reach a certain size in Finland or 75 years in Newfoundland could reach the same size in seven years in Central Africa, Venezuela or New Guinea. Venezuela has 120 million acres of forest land, but imports vast quantities of timber; this is economic absurdity. If a way could be found to grow a certain species of tree while keeping other species out, Venezuela would be much better off.

Finally, it should always be remembered that trees provide food, not only in the fruit that they bear, but in their very fibre. The Swedes during World War II ate food made from wood pulp, and current experiments indicate that several good bulky foods can be made from pulp. We cannot afford to ignore any single source of food.

197

14   PESTS; ANIMAL AND FOWL DISEASES

If there are many ways of gaining more food, there is one way in which the world can stop losing so much of it. This is by pest and disease control. In one recent year the loss to pests of food actually in store was 85,600,000 tons, enough to feed for a year every tenth person alive. The United States is the best example, for here storage conditions are certainly equal to the best in the world and pest control is practised. Nevertheless, rats destroy each year seven million metric tons of grain, while insect pests destroy up to another 16 million metric tons. The F.A.O. estimates that throughout the world about 35 million tons of grain are lost to pests each year—a staggering figure, equivalent in the developing countries to 25 per cent of the available food. F.A.O. further estimates that nine million tons of protein per annum could be saved by preventing cereal grain being destroyed by insects and rodents; this is greater than the current annual output of oil seed protein.

Ritchie Calder has claimed that, on a world scale, food field pests are consuming food equal to 10 times what would be necessary to provide rations for the annual increase in population.

The losses are equivalent to the produce of tens of millions of hectares and most could be prevented at a cost very small in relation to the crops saved. Such chemicals as D.D.T. have greatly increased yield of fruit and vegetables, but this and other chemicals are rarely used outside North America, Western Europe and Oceania.

Illogically, pest control is regarded as a 'negative' aspect of food production and little loan or grant money is available for projects and pesticides. Apart from the F.A.O. most of the work is left to semi-official organizations and to the harassed labours of scattered officials.

Locusts are one of the great menaces, producing plagues that have to be seen to be believed. The females lay their eggs—or rather spear them into the ground—at a rate of 2,000 to the square foot. These eggs produce locusts numerous enough to gather in swarms up to 75 square miles in area. Flying at speeds of over 40 miles an hour they cover up to 1,000 miles a day, and when they alight their mass overwhelms each acre with a weight of 700 tons.

The arrival of a locust swarm is a terrifying sight, for the mass of bodies—each locust has a five-inch wingspan—blots out the sun and is ominous with its noise. A swarm may alight on a man-high field of flourishing crops; when it leaves only a few bare stalks remain.

Some countries remain locust-free for years and then have a plague, such as happened to India and Pakistan in 1962, when 30 swarms invaded India and more than 50 devastated Pakistan. Even in normal years there is not enough food; after a locust infestation there is famine.

Other countries have had years of infestation but on a limited scale, such as Borneo since 1958. The Philippines need to control their locusts regularly but Malaya, though suffering from the very large Bombay locust from time to time, is able to keep them under control by knowing the breeding grounds and by chemical spraying of swarms when they appear. Large areas of West Africa are now under control as well, but the migratory desert locust remains a scourge for East Africa, the Red Sea, Middle Asia and the Persian Gulf, and by virtue of the manner in which locusts swarm and travel Pakistan and India suffer most from these huge insects. Their threat is another constant menace to people always on the edge of total starvation.

The Anti-Locust Research Centre in London, founded in 1929 and reinforced since 1945 with F.A.O. and United Nations Special Fund money, has been able to do much to forecast and check outbreaks. One of the major problems for the loosely constructed inter-area organizations is to persuade some countries to use part of their limited anti-locust funds to fight a potential swarm.

Country A might be well aware that a swarm is breeding but reckons that it will depart without causing any harm—or it gambles on this possibility. So it spends no money on wiping out the swarm. Apart from being mean this is also shortsighted, for after flying to another area to breed these locusts could leave offspring which will return to plague Country A.

The difficulty of locating a breeding ground is great. For instance, one traditional ground is the Rajasthan Desert of India, covering 80,000 square miles. In an area this size thorough plans are needed to spot and scotch a swarm. Nearly 60 observation posts are scattered about the desert and locust control teams have more than 200 vehicles and five aircraft for patrolling. The danger is so constantly serious that locust control officers have power to commandeer machines and to conscript men to fight an emergency.

The F.A.O. is involved in the fight against locusts, and a special team operates on the borders of Pakistan and India, with the primary object of studying locusts and trying to find better methods of dealing with them.

The olive fly, whose larva causes losses estimated at millions of pounds a year in Mediterranean countries, is another pest under attack. So, too, is the webworm which attacks fruit trees, and the sun pest, a critical problem in Iran, Iraq, Afghanistan, Turkey, North Africa, Syria and the Soviet Union. In the first warm days of spring these insects migrate from their mountainous winter hideouts and attack cereal crops in the valleys. Externally the grains show no sign of damage, but the seeds are unsuitable for making bread. The F.A.O. hopes to find a solution. But the work of a few experts, no matter how dedicated and clever, is inadequate in volume and can have no great influence until people are better educated.

Despite the justifiable fears of Professor McMillan and others about the pending shortage of water for livestock, the possibility of increasing the supply of livestock products —at least in short term—are better than those of increasing crop yields. The U.S. Department of Agriculture predicts, for example, that a single cow will produce as many as 1,000 calves in its lifetime, compared to the present 10, through the use of hormones which will keep the cycle of ovulation and pregnancy in cows and other domestic animals under exact control. Embryos will be transferred from special breeder animals to ordinary incubator animals. There will be substantial increases in prolificacy of a herd and a radical improvement in quality animal production. Similarly, says the Department, milk production will soar to 30,000 lb. a cow from today's 8,000.

At present, though, animal and fowl diseases are making great inroads into the potential quality available.

Losses from some of these diseases are climbing steeply as they spread to areas not previously affected. For instance, until the last decade horse sickness was confined to East and South Africa. Since then it has spread to Israel, Lebanon, Cyprus, Iran, Iraq, Jordan, Pakistan, Turkey, Syria.

A vaccine is available, but so many millions of horses, donkeys and mules would need to be treated that the task would be hopelessly difficult. Still, the vaccine can be used to check spread of the disease. Pigs and their owners are not so lucky: no vaccine has been developed against swine fever, which killed 120,000 pigs in Spain and 16,000 in Portugal in a recent year. Most of this number were slaughtered to prevent spread of the disease. The economic loss is great, while the loss of protein from people's diet is even more serious as more than 50 per cent of the meat eaten by poorer people is pork.

The economic loss from animal diseases is also great and sometimes so serious that they can ruin a country. In Burma during the war of 1939–45 rinderpest killed about a million cattle. Most of them were work beasts, the only source of power by which farmers could cultivate their land. Burma consequently had no rice to export; this not only strained her economy to breaking point but caused famine in neighbouring Bengal; children had no milk and there was a shortage of dung for heating and cooking. In 1951–3 a foot-and-mouth disease epidemic in Europe cost £150 million, of which Britain's share was £2½ million. But this was cheap compared with the mastitis which costs the British dairy industry about £10 million a year. The same disease costs the United States nearly £75 million annually. Lungworm disease in livestock costs Britain a further £3 million a year. In one year Western Europe lost 15 per cent of its animals by disease, a monetary setback of £600 million.

However, F.A.O. specialists believe that most of the serious diseases which attack livestock in the underdeveloped countries could now not merely be controlled but eliminated. For example, the rinderpest which killed two million cattle a year five years ago is now virtually eliminated.

Ranikhet or 'Newcastle disease' kills 70 to 100 per cent of poultry flocks in the Far East, thus making poultry farming an economically ruinous and discouraging occupation. New and cheap vaccines can overcome the problem and have already done so in Singapore, where poultry numbers jumped from 600,000 to seven million in seven years; egg production has gone up 1,000 per cent and poultry farming is now a commercial industry. Similar programmes are showing effectiveness in other parts of Malaysia, in Thailand, Indonesia and Japan. Disease-controlled poultry production in China, India, Pakistan, Egypt, Turkey and other places could result in more food for everybody. Naturally, it is not so simple as that. Somebody will have to give these people the fowls and the vaccines and teach them how to keep fowls and use the vaccines. Until a general rise in the standard of living takes place so that people can afford to pay for fowls and eggs, the government might need to subsidize the industry. Countries with little space for fowl runs could well study the example of Japan. Every square yard of farm land is vital in Japan and little is available for fowls, so the Japanese have built circular multi-storey chicken houses. Open to the sun but protected from the rain, these 'fowl flats' are so designed that one person can easily maintain a number of them.

Control of haemorrhaic septicaemia and the tsetse fly is not yet effective, but it will assuredly become so. Victory over the tsetse fly will open up vast areas of otherwise suitable cattle country in Africa.

Countries with a healthy, diversified and resilient economic backgound can withstand losses from stock diseases and can recover from them fairly quickly. But in poorer countries disease among animals could be catastrophic. If the supply of animal products is to be increased by the necessary 300 per cent by the year 2000, animal diseases must be effectively controlled through international co-operation and education. The F.A.O. has achieved much, but all efforts have not eradicated foot-and-mouth disease from Europe or horse sickness from the Middle East and Africa.

Fungi adds to the loss. Modern methods of crop and grain storage and transport are used by only a fraction of the world's population. If some of the developing nations spent a quarter of what is now going into arms on improved storage and transport they could give their peoples much more food.

15 FERTILIZERS; NEW SEEDS; MECHANIZATION

Better fertilizers and far more widespread use of them, improved seeds and plants, greater mechanization and use of chemicals are other factors in the fight against time to produce more food. Because of expense, mechanization must wait for years in some areas, and the use of chemicals can be deterred, but a lot could be done almost at once with more intensive and extensive use of fertilizers and better seeds. Unfortunately, no aspect of food production stands alone, and in large areas of the world inadequate use of fertilizers and better seeds is linked with low standards of education.

Japan once again provides the best example of the influence fertilizers can have on a country's economy. When she became prosperous she put so much money and research into fertilizing that she now wins 35 cwt. of rice and 17 cwt. of wheat to the acre. Comparative Indian figures are 10 cwt. and $5\frac{1}{2}$ cwt. This latter figure is equal to what was reaped in England in medieval times.

Not that Great Britain is without soil fertility worries. Sir Albert Howard, in an address at Oxford, noted that, 'By far the most important demand of the Industrial Revolution was the creation of two new hungers—the hunger of a rapidly increasing urban population and the hunger of its machines. Both needed the things raised on the land; both have seriously depleted the reserves of fertility in our soils. Neither of these hungers has been accompanied by the return of these respective wastes to the land. Instead, vast sums were spent in completely side-tracking these wastes and preventing their return to the land which so sorely needed them. Much ingenuity was devoted to developing an effective method of removing the human wastes to the rivers and seas. These finally took the shape of our waterborne sewage system. The contents of the dustbins of house and factory first found their way into huge dumps and then into incinerators or into refuse tips sealed by a thin layer of cinders or oil.'

He meant, of course, that waste capable of making humus should be returned to the soil to enrich it.

In India the fields distant from any village are much less fertile than those near the village; this is because the closer ones have benefited from deposition of wastes and ashes and from human and animal excreta. A human habitation occupied for any length of time acquires increasing fertility, often inadvertently.

The wide use of fertilizers depends on a knowledge of the soil itself, again a matter for education. If every farmer realized that every ton of wheat represents four-fifths of a ton of soil removed from his land with its integrated nutrients, they might be more willing to buy the idea of fertilizers. In effect, vast quantities of topsoil are constantly being moved from one country to another or from rural areas to cities. Grain fed to stock—as is the corn of the United States' corn belt—is returned to the earth as farmyard manure, but owing to modern sewage the greater quantity of food eaten by city dwellers is lost to the land.

The F.A.O. believes that by crop rotation and use of fertilizers alone production could be increased by at least 50 per cent and in many countries by 100 per cent. World production of fertilizers has much more than doubled since 1948. It has risen well above 100 per cent in Asia, but this is mostly in Japan. The rest of Asia collectively used only 500,000 tons annually. Europe and North America account for 60 per cent of world production. Production of nitrogen fertilizer has reached 12 million tons a year but is still one of the most under-exploited discoveries of all time.

Inducing farmers in backward countries to use fertilizers consistently is a disappointing task, as the Indian National Council for Applied Economic Research implied in a report. 'It was surprising to note that though a number of farmers had positive experience with fertilizers they were not fully convinced about the efficacy of their continued use. The existing information and promotional agencies have thus not succeeded in bringing about basic changes in the attitude of most farmers.'

This is rather unreasonable because most Indian farmers are subsistence farmers with nothing to sell; therefore they cannot buy fertilizer. Even if the Indian had a crop to exchange for fertilizer, the average Indian probably would not be interested because he can see no positive return.

Nevertheless, in other areas farming owes the fertilizer industry a debt which it is repaying by buying more fertilizer. The industry unshackled agriculture, because it eliminated the need to take nutrients from one field to another. Because, so far, it is a bulky product, fertilizer is not the whole answer and a farmer must take transport costs into consideration. Great Britain uses much fertilizer because distances are short, a limited amount of land is under the plough and there is a great urban population and market. Australia, however, with dissimilar conditions, relies mainly on leguminous plants for improving the soil's nitrogen content.

Some low-productivity countries—which are also those which most urgently need high productivity—could not be immediately aided even by limitless amounts of fertilizer. This is a point that well-meaning but uninformed enthusiasts often forget. Hundreds of thousands of square miles of peasant farmland have been exploited to the point of exhaustion or have been so thoroughly leached by millions of years of weathering that the land cannot respond to simple fertilizer treatment. In the tropics inter-action of fertilizers and water supply is paramount, whereas it is insignificant in the temperate regions. Similarly, the fertile temperate lands respond readily to fertilizers. It is just another pathetic paradox in the hunger story.

Fertilizers *are* used on sugar and tea, both tropical crops and, significantly, both economically linked with the industrial and wealthy West. Since larger crops will bring in more money, the growers will naturally spend some of their money on ways of increasing yield.

Finding the key to high productivity in tropical areas is not easy, but when found the results can be spectacular. There has been no well-documented case concerning food, but the experiments made by a British expert, D. A. Lawes, with cotton in Northern Nigeria show what could be achieved with food. Farmers in this region were obtaining only 150 lb.–200 lb. per acre, although small-scale experiments by Lawes and others showed that 600 lb. could be expected, if better seeds were planted at more suitable time with the use of fertilizers. Lawes prepared a high-fertility plot on which he achieved a yield of 2,000 lb. per acre, maintaining or improving on it for five years.

All soils, even the most unresponsive, can eventually be made to yield. In Uganda one stubborn area resisted normal fertilizer dressings, but finally gave high yields following the addition of organic manure mixed with nitrogen phosphate, calcium and sulphur. But technical solution is only one part of the answer—so the developing countries are even poorer in industrial resources, including fertilizer factories, than they are in agriculture. How are they to obtain the massive quantities of fertilizer needed? Only by achieving a better balanced economy, including, sooner or later, their own fertilizer industry. When they can do this the farmers can feed their own urban areas, peopled by people working in industries which supply the farmer with what he wants. This is the true and only practical solution—the wedding of agriculture with industry. In the meantime money spent on extolling the virtue of fertilizers would not be wasted. Professor Borgstrom of Michigan University estimates that before the end of the century over 700 million metric tons of fertilizer will need to be produced and transported every year.

Hand in hand with fertilizers goes the breeding, selection and hybridization of seeds, all of which could greatly increase production. Plant breeding techniques can develop varieties with a higher ability to produce or with stronger resistance to disease, pests and extreme climate. Selection involves choosing for use the best that already exists. Hybridization creates new types through genetic combinations.

Perhaps only the F.A.O. fully realizes the dramatic changes that can be brought about by using better seed. They rate it so highly that since 1957 they have had a World Seed Campaign and in 1960 they fostered a World Seed Year. The organization's own successes have been illustrative enough. By 'selling' Yugoslavia the idea of using Italian wheat the F.A.O. increased the Yugoslav yield by 30 per cent and the country is now wheat self-sufficient. In the developed countries seed technology is extraordinarily developed, but the discoveries are not being transferred rapidly enough to the countries which need them most. The developed countries are willing to share their discoveries, but the task of inducing peasant and primitive farmers to adopt them is long, tedious and at times heart-breaking.

In the backward countries the scope for improvement is immense. Some types of plants should be discarded and replaced with better-yielding varieties. So much could already be done, but man is a conservative animal, resistant to change. Of course, many farmers do not know of improved varieties, in most places improved seed is hard to get and perhaps dearer to buy, and some requires more care and perhaps a particular type of fertilizer.

N. W. Pirie suggests that work should be well under way in breeding and selecting new species of plants (and animals) adapted to environments that are at present used inadequately. However, many new organizations would be needed to spread these benefits to the wet tropics. Pirie proposes institutes of food technology which would reverse the usual concept of agriculture, and having found out which plants grow best in an environment, would try to find ways of making something useful from them. He suggests oilseed residues, leafy crops and roots at present regarded as unpalatable or even as uneatable. He is being quite realistic when he says that these things could be made into useful food by biochemical engineering processes.

The use of the correct strain of a plant for a particular area is once again well shown in the case of Japan, which has a much higher rice yield per acre than anywhere else in Asia. This is because Japan grows Japonica rice, which yields 2,352 lb. to the acre, while the Inica variety grown by most other countries, especially in the tropics, yields less than a third of this. Admittedly, Japonica will not so far grow well in the tropical regions, but F.A.O. experts, working in India and Ceylon, are developing new strains which combine the best qualities of both types. This is an example of how food institutes could help quality and quantity of production. At present, when a new area is opened up, man-the-conservative tends to grow familiar foods in it. But if he is to survive he must reverse his concepts about agriculture; he must discover which plants grow best and make new foods from them. Pirie's food institutes could set the lead in this.

However, once again it is a case of the advanced countries advancing even further while the backward ones become even more backward. The position has become so ridiculously extreme that American farmers can select from an array of 50,000 chemical preparations to help them in their work. There are fungicides and pesticides, chemicals to condition the soil and to treat seeds before planting. There are even defoliants to make the leaves fall off so that the crop is easy to harvest. The whole of the Indian sub-continent has only one company selling chemical preparations—and it is a small company.

Anybody who has seen a peasant farmer toiling behind a simple wooden plough pulled by a horse, ox, bullock or water buffalo will have felt sympathy for him. The weather is usually very hot and the soil is extremely hard or equally muddy. The ploughshare makes practically no impact on hard ground and any piece of work takes a long time. I once spent a day in Libya labouring with pick and mattock on stony, barren-looking ground. Together, my host and I dug up an area the size of an average English garden, and it was superficially dug at that. This particular farmer had not even a hand plough because he could not afford an animal to pull it. There seems to be a misconception that mechanization is merely a means of saving work. 'What would be the use of every Indian having a motor plough?' a traveller once asked me in an aircraft over India. 'The average farm is so small the farmer has plenty of time to plough it by traditional methods. What would he do with his time if a motor plough could do the job in a day?'

Well, he might have time to go to school—when adult schools are widespread enough. The point is that a mechanized plough does the job so much better; it breaks the soil thoroughly and deeply. It is not necessary for every Indian to have such a plough; often one to a village would be sufficient.

There are some interesting views on mechanization. A French economist, M. de Jouvenal, said, 'The United States became mechanized because it was a country of high wages, and these high wages were due to high productivity in agriculture. It is quite stupid to seek to introduce mechanization through gifts from outside and to raise wages by decree, instead of using the natural method which is to increase productivity in food growing.'*

But productivity depends largely on mechanization. Now mechanization is perhaps a misleading word, for the tendency is to use it as the Americans or New Zealanders use it, to mean powered machinery. Much can be done by simply having better tools, as the F.A.O. so dramatically showed in Afghanistan.

The scheme was a classic of its type, for here tools and their use were practically unknown. When the F.A.O. experts first went to the country they found that because of economic and other difficulties power mechanization was impracticable. The country had a large horse population, so these animals were used to pull light ploughs. The F.A.O. men introduced and had manufactured locally seed drills, light hoes, scythes, threshers and seed cleaners. The result was increased yield of cotton, wheat and sugar beet through improved tillage, better weed control and speedier harvesting. The agricultural economy of the country and the increased mechanical ability of the Afghans has since resulted in the introduction of machines.

The F.A.O. has been the guiding force and in some cases the inspiration behind other mechanization projects in Libya, Morocco, Tunisia, Egypt and Ceylon. The Gal Oya Valley in Ceylon is one of the most successful projects.

* In a lecture to the French Employers Federation, January 1957.

About 50 villages, each with 150 families trained to use better equipment, were the crux of the scheme. They have drastically changed the rice situation in the dry zones of Ceylon. In 1952 the farmers of the Gal Oya Valley could only meet local demands; now they export over a million bushels. As part of the same scheme water grass was imported from Africa to increase livestock farming.

In addition, pulses, maize, cotton, vegetables, are being grown in the area and a livestock industry, founded on water grass imported from Africa, is flourishing. More than 14,000 acres are now under sugar and the cane will be processed locally. If this sort of scheme will work in Ceylon it will work elsewhere, though perhaps not with the same speed, as the Cingalese learn quickly.

What can be achieved by power mechanization was never more vividly shown by an individual than in the case of a Canadian farmer, Varno Westersund, who runs, by himself, a farm of 2,750 acres in Alberta. He uses hired help only at harvesting. Westersund's methods are based on maximum use of farming machinery. He has a machine that can cultivate or seed 30 to 40 acres in an hour; he uses a special cultivator which allows the residue and surface waste from previous crops to remain in place on top of land to prevent erosion. He sprays his crops from the air. Westersund's farm averages 20 to 40 bushels of wheat to the acre and 10 to 20 bushels of flax, but he also raises oats, barley and grass seed and runs cattle, pigs and chickens. As a scientific farmer Westersund keeps crop, rainfall and production records.

It might not be desirable for farms in India, for example, to reach such a high standard of mechanization, but fewer farmers producing more food could lead to increased standards of living all round.

The ability of power mechanization to invigorate the economy is most clearly shown by New Zealand, where machines are reaching towards the ultimate. Mechanization was a matter of survival here, because New Zealand, with

213

her markets 12,000 miles away, had to produce her butter, cheese and lamb in competition with Denmark, Holland and France, with markets on their doorstep.

Until mechanization is widespread and not merely the luxury of the privileged few, food production cannot reach its necessary volume. I am aware of the difficulties, but it seems to me that enough use has not been made of the many successful mechanization schemes. Perhaps once again, this is because of the difficulty of communication with illiterate people.

Every year a vast amount of farm machinery, still in good working order, is discarded and replaced in the advanced countries. Plant is frequently replaced to reduce wage costs and to gain tax benefits. What happens to all this 'old' machinery? So far, there is only one organization to provide secondhand machinery for underdeveloped countries, and that is a private one set up by a Swedish businessman, Mr. Langenskold. Enough secondhand machinery finding its way, free or at the cost of transport, to Africa, India, Asia Minor and South America could help to increase food production. It could, indeed, so increase standards of living that farmers would be able to buy new machinery from the industrial countries. Instead of building observatories in Chile the West Germans might consider using available money to ship their thousands of discarded farm machines to that country.

Again, we can so easily overdo things and cause ourselves and posterity much trouble. Plans for increased food production involve large-scale efforts to modify the environment, but the dangers of such modification are great, and often unrecognized. In 1968 the realistic Paul Ehrlich was predicting that the rate of soil deterioration would accelerate as the food crisis intensifies, that 'ecology will be ignored more and more as things get tough'. He was referring to over-use of pesticides and fertilizers, to over-cropping, forest clearance. Pesticides, he points out, often create pests. Careless over-use of D.D.T. for instance, has put into the pest category many species of mites. The insects which ate the mites were killed by D.D.T. but the mites were resistant to D.D.T. Of course, the chemical companies can make miticides, but Ehrlich claims that some of the more potent miticides seem to be powerful carcinogens—cancer-producing substances. Pesticide pollution is a major world problem. D.D.T. residues have been found in the fat deposits of eskimos, Antarctic penguins and Antarctic seals. Concentrations in the fat deposits of Americans average 11 parts per million, in Israelis 19.2 per million. Dr. M. M. Hargraves, Senior Consultant of the Mayo Clinic, New York, says that deaths from use of pesticides in the U.S. exceed those caused by road accidents.

16 NEW WAYS AND MEANS

A great many relatively minor things could be done to increase food production, to distribute it more equitably or to make new foods more acceptable. Some of these things are being done and will, in due course, have their impact. A few have already had considerable influence, in some cases without the public being aware of it.

Technology has achieved much and has reached such a stage that, strictly speaking, soil is not even needed. The United States has at least 100 nutricultural or hydroponic farms where crops are grown in chemical solutions without soil. Hydroponics have a big future. No chemical introduced into the human system by these crops is harmful.

Is it still too soon to tackle the problem of creating synthetic foods? Let us look at a basic factor in the global equation of food and people: the needs of the individual human being in terms of nourishment.

Apart from water, man needs five groups of basic elements

216

—proteins, carbohydrates, fats, vitamins and mineral salts. As daily nourishment, an adult should have, on average, two litres of water, 80–100 grammes of protein, 400–500 grammes of carbohydrates and 80–100 grammes of fats. As for vitamins (0.1 gr. a day, excluding choline, of which 0.1 gr. is also needed) and salts (20 gr. in all, including 10 gr. of cooking salt), the needs are small and can be easily met.

Synthetic foods must obviously include all the indispensable salts and vitamins which are already being produced on a large scale through chemical and microbiological processes. And with the present industrial manufacture of vitamins, it is clear that man has already entered the age of artificial, non-agricultural production of nutritious substances.

The role of the other three groups of elements is to provide the human system with energy and 'building materials'. The first function is largely carried out by carbohydrates and fats and the second by proteins. Here we have a major distinction between groups of nutritious substances.

The carbohydrates and fats which provide energy are burned up during assimilation and lose their original chemical identity. Certain components of these two groups are interchangeable and the groups themselves can largely be replaced and transformed one into the other, by the human organism.

Proteins are completely different. Turned into amino acids by the digestive system, they provide the body with the 'bricks' which it needs to build its own proteins, of which 8 out of a total of 20 (9 in the case of children) are indispensable. Food should contain all these amino acids in strictly controlled proportions. Proteins are thus the most expensive and deficient items in our human diet, their most valuable and rarest elements being the indispensable group of amino acids.

Any pronounced protein deficiency, particularly if due to the absence in the diet of one or more indispensable amino

217

acids, results in specific vitamin deficiency diseases such as *kwashiorkor*. Once restored, the missing amino acid re-establishes the balance and leads to a striking increase in the nutritive value of many proteins of vegetable origin.

The problem is reduced to either the microbiological synthesis of protein or the microbiological or chemical synthesis of amino acids which can then be used, in suitable doses, in the composition of synthetic diets.

Such synthetic diets, consisting of amino acids, vitamins, minerals, glucose and linoleic acid ether, have been prepared by a U.S. scientist, Dr. Milton Winitz, and tested on human beings over extended periods. They are used especially in the intravenous feeding of patients who, for one reason or another, cannot be fed normally.

Here we have a true model of synthetic nutriment. Apart from its strictly medical application, its real significance is in showing that it is possible to be nourished by a proper mixture of synthetic substances each ingredient of which can be obtained by synthesis.

Unfortunately the cost price of many of them is still prohibitive. Produced on a large scale and by more efficient methods their price could easily be reduced, as has been the case with methionine, lysine and glutamic acid, the annual world production of which now exceeds 100,000 tons at a price of only one pound per kilogramme.

If all the other amino acids were manufactured at the same price, the daily needs per person would be met for about 30p. There is no reason why the reduction in cost could not be even greater—the present technique of producing amino acids, which is based on the cheap substance, nitromethane, seems very promising.

The Institute of Elementary Organic Compounds of the U.S.S.R. Academy of Sciences and the Pedagogical Institute of Leningrad, among other research institutes, have developed the synthesis of all the amino acids from this substance. No less encouraging possibilities are offered by the microbiological method, especially if the micro-organisms which produce amino acids can be switched from carbohydrate foods to hydrocarbons. A number of achievements in this direction have already been recorded.

Apart from agriculture, another technique exists for the production of proteins on an industrial scale—that provided by microbiology. Scientists in a number of countries—including France, U.K. and U.S.S.R.—are already working on the production of fodder yeasts for which the raw material is provided by paraffins, one of the cheapest by-products of petroleum. Hydrocarbon yeasts is exceptionally rich in protein. It contains over 40 per cent compared with the 30 per cent protein content of soya beans, the most nourishing of all agricultural products.

The French scientist, Alfred Champagnat, director of a Marseilles laboratory specializing in this research, was first to draw attention to the extraordinary possibilities of these yeasts in making up for the present protein deficiency: 'The annual world shortage of animal protein can be estimated at three million tons. This corresponds to 15 million tons of beef cattle. For an annual production of 1,000 million tons of petroleum it can be assumed that 700 million tons are paraffin based. The production of 7 million tons of protein-vitamin concentrate, equivalent to 3 million tons of protein, would consume only 1 per cent of these 700 million tons of petroleum.'

Why is it that researchers are more interested in food for human consumption than in animal fodder? Here again, figures provide an explanation. Six million tons of synthetic protein are required annually to meet the needs of 250 million people; to nourish the same number of people with protein produced by stock farming would require the production of from 50 to 100 million tons of dehydrated protein to feed the animals themselves.

This is the problem facing chemists: Is it possible to transform a daily diet consisting of 100 grammes of protein,

219

450 grammes of carbohydrates and 100 grammes of fats into food which, far from being less good and less varied, is even better and more varied than the usual fare? In other words, the problem is one of taste, smell and consistency.

In their original state, practically all natural proteins are odourless and tasteless. The same applies to starchy macromolecular carbohydrates and to fats. It is what is added to and mixed with our food which gives it a special smell and taste, and especially the substances formed in the process of cooking.

The taste of any substance can be broken down into four main categories—sweet, salty, sour and bitter—which we identify through the taste-buds on our tongue. If we consider taste separately from smell, it is clear that any taste can be reproduced by a suitable addition of say, sugar, salt, acid and caffeine.

However, the question of smell is a much more delicate problem because smell combines with taste to form flavour, which is really what makes food appetizing. In our everyday fare, flavour is obtained by heating or the addition of local spices (onion, garlic, paprika, parsley, celery) or tropical ones (pepper, ginger, cloves, etc.).

The action of these substances is well known and corresponds to a simple principle. The effect of heating food is to form a mixture of substances giving off an attractive odour formed by dozens of volatile ingredients of which only a few are responsible for the specific smell. This aroma can be reconstituted either by mixing the same quantity of ingredients or by heating certain amino acids and their mixtures with different sugars.

The smell is enhanced when an unsaturated fatty acid is added to the mixture of amino acids. The characteristic odour of boiled beef or chicken casserole can be obtained in this way. Adding a trace of trimethylamino oxide produces the smell of salt-water fish, and amino valeric adelhyde imitates the smell of boiled fresh-water fish.

220

The final problem is that of the consistency of food. A variety of methods exist for making sophisticated imitations of standard human foods from synthetic proteins. In the United States, certain firms are selling and promoting, with great commercial subtlety, soya protein products which simulate various parts of chickens and different cuts of beef. A Russian institute has developed a technique for making sturgeon caviar, the quality of which is practically indistinguishable from the real thing. Already in Britain, in 1971, 5,000 tons of vegetable protein were consumed, heavily disguised as sausages, tinned meat, beef, hamburgers, etc.

However, a considerable amount of research has still to be done on natural food substitutes. Recent investigation on vegetable-protein 'meat', by Dr. Michael Crawford of the Nuffield Institute of Comparative Medicine in London, has demonstrated that we get far more than just protein out of animal flesh. The most vital 'extras' are the structural fats of the phospholipid group which are contained within genuine animal meat cells. These fats are absolutely essential for the development of brain and central nervous tissue (they make up over 60 per cent of the dry matter of the human brain) and they cannot be obtained from plants and cannot be synthesized by man. As a high proportion of our brain tissue is formed when we are in the womb or during the first five years of our life, it would obviously be unwise to deprive pregnant women or young children of an adequate supply of phospholipids.

Imagine the day when a country's economy is based on the manufacture of synthetic food instead of on traditional methods of food production. A few factories, sited in different parts of the country where coal and petroleum are to be found, prepare all the food required by the population. Altogether, these factories occupy barely a few hundred square miles. Agriculture with its need for a vast labour force and its limited capacity for progress could be abolished, with the exception perhaps of market gardens and horticulture.

There would no longer be any need for the vast industry which formerly provided agriculture with its equipment— tractors, machines, tools, nor for the metal used in making them, nor for the fuel used to power them, nor for chemical fertilizers, pesticides, etc. A large proportion of the population previously engaged in these industries and in agriculture itself is thus freed for more productive work. Only a minute part of this manpower is needed for the production of synthetic food.

The way is open for the old food industry to give way to an entirely new industry, infinitely more compact: no more bad years, poor harvests, unproductive land, no more calamitous losses due to climate, natural catastrophes, parasites, plant diseases, all of which today still take their toll of a considerable part of every harvest.

It should be possible to develop food products, ready to eat, needing only to be heated, packaged or tinned like the products on sale today, but with the fundamental difference that they contain the normal amount of vitamins and essential components of natural food and have the highest nutritive value. Already the appearance of these dishes leave nothing to be desired and, with a standard composition (protein, carbohydrates, fats, salts, vitamins) adapted to each age need, these foods could be the best source of health and energy the human system can have, even better than the best natural products.

No more obesity, no more fatty degeneration of the heart, liver and other complaints of the kind. At the least sign of physical abnormality special diets can be composed.

All the conditions are to hand for the transformation of villages into towns and towns into garden cities. Vast tracts of land previously reserved for crop growing give way progressively to forests and parks. The silting and drying up of rivers is stopped and the abundance of food products leads to the solution of the world shortage of drinking water which is steadily worsening.*

Chemicals are playing such an extraordinary part in food preparation that the stage has been reached where there is really no such thing as a wholly natural commercial food. There are even entirely artificial foods on the market, completely produced in chemical factories. Artificial flavours are generally the taste Western people enjoy. If the whole United States strawberry crop were turned into natural flavouring it would satisfy only one medium-sized city for a year; the strawberry flavouring comes from such chemicals as ethyl methylphenyl, benzyl valerate, ethyl malonate and benzyl acetate. Caprioc acid gives the flavour of cheese, cyclohexyl acetate the tang of orange and butyric acid the flavour of butter. The latest estimate of the amount of chemicals used in the United States bread industry is 16 million lb. Still, it is easy to be unnecessarily overwhelmed and perhaps frightened by the array of chemical additives. Synthetic grape flavour has five chemicals, but natural grape flavour has 19 chemicals.

Retailed investigation of the effect of chemical additives is, of course, vital and stricter governmental control is needed so that public health can be safeguarded.

There is danger as well as hope in the immense number of artificial substitutes for true materials. The danger lies in the lessening need for imports from some backward countries. Natural rubber is still a major export for such countries as Malaya, Ceylon and Thailand, but polymerized isporene is a satisfactory synthetic replacement. An American tobacco firm, by impregnating its cigarette tips with

* This outline of synthetic foods is based on the research and field work of two leading Soviet specialists, Alexander Nesmeyanov and Vassily Belikov. Nesmeyanov was president of the U.S.S.R. Academy of Sciences and is founder and director of the Academy's Institute of Elementary Organic Compounds. Belikov is head of the laboratory for the synthesis of nutritional substances at Nesmeyanov's institute.

chemicals to give the taste of tobacco, has shown that there is no need to put tobacco beyond the tip, for anything that will burn could make up the bulk. In food, supermarket 'fresh' bread in packets is often made weeks before sale; the smell of newly-baked bread comes from the impregnated packing paper.

During the war of 1939–45 the Germans made ersatz (synthetic) coffee and tea and the neutral Swedes, unable to import as much food as necessary, produced a lot of food from wood. Now an American laboratory has developed a synthetic coffee aroma; the flavour and texture of cocoa will follow. Milk from soya beans is being made in quantity in Djakarta, capital of Indonesia. This is hopeful, because soya beans are the heaviest-yielding field crop, but its yield is small compared to that from the one-cell algin plant, chlorella; one acre in a year will produce 20 tons of protein and eight tons of fat.

In sugar-growing areas yeast factories are now producing 2,000 lbs. of protein from five tons of sugar, which is the yield of an acre. If food yeast could be made acceptable it could make a radical improvement in protein-shortage. Its importance can be gauged from the protein yield of beef cattle—50 lbs. an acre.

Making 'strange' foods acceptable is one of the challenges, and it can only be mastered by systematic education, and by giving these foods appealing tastes and smells, a mild deception justifiable in the emergency. All humanity must, sooner or later, become food-progressive. At present much valuable food is eaten only by the adventurous or so-called faddists.

Dandelions, for instance, are excellent in salads and can be cooked. The plantain can be made into an appetizing soup and is rich in vitamins and minerals. The unhappily named pigweed has been long ignored, but is similar to spinach, tastes better and is rich in iron and vitamins. Being a weed, it is hardy and grows all the year in some areas.

Amaranth, a type of pigweed, is pleasant when cooked, especially when mixed with chicory or cress. One weed, purslane, can be eaten raw, cooked or pickled; stems and leaves can all be eaten, and the seeds from the plant make a type of flour ideal for pancakes. Milkweed sprouts can be cooked like asparagus, while the unopened flower buds are cooked like broccoli; the buds and leaves can also be eaten. Plants such as these are not mere substitutes for the conventional vegetables; they are valuable and appetizing in their own right.

A long-range method of obtaining food is to open up the vast areas of cold lands in the north. This might seem sheer fantasy if the suggestion were made by anybody other than the F.A.O., but experts from this sober organization claim that 120,000 million hectares could be used. Difficulties exist, but the F.A.O. says, 'The land is there for man to transform if he will'. This applies to other areas mentioned elsewhere in this book—the tropical lands, the savannah regions, swamps.

A more immediate scheme is a permanent food first aid service, with stores at strategic places, to cope with such disasters as the drought-caused famine in East Africa in 1961.

Nearly 500,000 Africans in Kenya alone were starving and the death rate among livestock was 50 per cent. In Kenya a total of 352 Government and voluntary workers had to cover 68,000 square miles of territory. Their problem was aggravated by the great expense of delivering food to remote areas; it cost up to 75p to deliver one bag of maize. Tanganyika's experience during the same crisis showed that seed banks should also exist, for the famine ended with torrential rain and Tanganyika's main problem was to obtain seed to sow before the rain ceased and the land dried up again.

Crises uncover many weaknesses in the food situation, and not the least of them is human inefficiency and indifference. Again, India is a useful example. In the summer of 1964 India was gripped by famine and Australia offered her a million tons of wheat, if India could pick it up—a reasonable condition. If India had been prepared to use her military air fleet to ferry the wheat from Australia she could have broken the famine, but military requirements were allowed to come before the lives of ordinary people, many of whom died.

Except for Russia and China about a fifth of the world's what is grown for export. In any normal year the four main exporting countries—Canada, Argentina, Australia and the U.S.A.—hold in store nearly enough for two years' exports, a reasonably sized bank that could be used in cases of famine or flood emergency. A food bank of some kind would have been useful to cope with the problem of feeding the 5,500,000 East Pakistanis forced by civil war to flee to India in mid-1971. But communications must be adequate and government policy humane enough to deal with withdrawals from such a bank.

Nations and people are always ready to spring to the help of heart-appeal emergencies—the East Pakistan exodus for example—but it seems they cannot be stirred by an emergency that continues for years and decades. And if a nation is indifferent to the sufferings of its own people how can it expect foreigners to be moved to practical expressions of sympathy?

One common food not developed as widely as it might be is the potato, which could well be grown in greater quantities. The potato is best suited to a cool temperate climate, but of a world production of 280 million tons nearly 240 million tons are grown in Europe. This means that large parts of the Americas, Australia and New Zealand and probably parts of eastern Russia could grow much larger quantities of potatoes—if the object is merely to feed people. If profit is the motive then potato production in these countries will not increase, for they are low-priced and transport costs are heavy. However, they can be dried and concentrated and made into soup powder, which when cooked is filling and nutritious.

British scientists of the Tropical Products Institute have developed a new loaf which contains less than two-thirds wheat, in response to a growing demand from the developing countries.

The new loaf came into being because of a demand created by the social changes in those countries, the growth of urbanization being a main factor.

As a staple food bread has many advantages. It can be mass produced, will keep for several days and it is easy to distribute. In addition, it is an ideal material for enrichment with vitamins, minerals and protein concentrates. It can be used as an emergency food source in areas which have been devastated by natural disasters and where people are living at below subsistence levels. However, the traditional loaf, a valuable protein food, is made from wheat which does not readily grow in tropical and sub-tropical areas; its importation imposes a drain on badly-needed foreign exchange. The new loaf significantly reduces the amount used of North American and Russian wheats which are normally imported by the developing countries for making bread. It permits the inclusion of tropical cereals such as sorghum, millet, maize or rice or root crops such as cassava.

Co-operative schemes are among the most fruitful and humanly satisfying. Farmers taking part in such schemes have lower costs, higher profits, greater productivity and the use of co-operative facilities, such as farm machinery. There is nothing new about such schemes in the wealthier developed countries. Denmark and New Zealand among others, have shown that co-operative farming leads to greater output and efficiency, but they are unknown in many poorer areas. A small but excellent example has been working well in Ecuador since 1960. In the poverty-stricken area of San Pablo del Lago a priest, Dr. Justicia, founded an 800-acre co-operative, which now feeds and employs 6,000 people. The scheme has dairy cattle, sheep, pigs and poultry and also farms fish in Lake San Pablo. Aberdare, South Wales, has adopted the scheme and helps to finance it. If a lone inspired man can achieve such success, how much more widespread could the benefits be if organized on a large scale.

The Aberdare adoption of the San Pablo del Lago project is typical of a worthwhile food activity. Various local committees for the Freedom from Hunger campaign have greatly helped projects in many countries. By adopting a particular scheme or effort a community in a prosperous country can more readily identify itself with the people it is helping. Because of this funds are easier to raise and the recipient town or village is more directly appreciative. It is a people-to-people scheme and therefore is more human. The money is, naturally, much more limited, but the dividends in goodwill are greater than those which follow a massive monetary injection by some international organization.

17 THE CHOICE FOR MANKIND

Mankind has now reached a strange position: science can save a child's life much more readily than it can ensure that the child will be fed for life. Again, science is making great leaps into space but apparently cannot realize that there is no escape in space for mankind. Other planets cannot support our type of life, nor can we hope to bring food back from them.

Nobody can make a truly accurate prediction about the food future, because food does not depend merely on farming. Economic, political, social and cultural influences all obtrude. However, the F.A.O. is confident that humanity *need not* be starved out of existence, though it does not go so far as to say that this *will not* happen.

The trouble is that all the activity aimed at fighting the problem is not nearly enough. Well-fed countries and people simply do not realize the magnitude of the crisis. They are acting as if by contributing their two million pounds or two pounds to a relief organization, the mildly distressing situation will go away. But we are facing no passing crisis; we must accept the situation as a fact of life as much with us now and henceforth as is the nuclear bomb. We should do all we can now, while we look at the future imaginatively and with vision, planning an even grander—much grander —assault on the hunger front.

As the years pass an entirely new situation confronts us, due to the increase in population which has already taken place and which, unless checked, will mount with horrifying volume. The direct result is a radical change in the age structure of the population. In 1970 roughly 41 per cent of the population of the underdeveloped world were under 15 years old. In Costa Rica 50 per cent are under this age. Overall, about half the entire population of the underdeveloped world is under 20. This predominance of youth has a profound influence on attitudes and education; unrest and discontent will become more intensive and extensive.

At the same time the world's power centres will continue to move. In 1950 the United States was the undisputed centre of world power; now she can barely justify the title 'leader of the free world'. The Soviet Union has come up, but Western Europe as an entity is more powerful than both and inevitably China will become more potent.

It is quite possible that China will feel forced to launch a third world war in a frantic effort to find food for its masses. Most of humanity might be destroyed in the process but those who survive will be able to start again, with enough food to go around.

Such a war could be disastrous, especially in the length of time needed for recovery. Industrial economy might well be unable to recover and people all over the world would revert to an ancient agrarian economy. What a triumph this would be for Thomas Malthus and his doctrines!

Western liberalism is, perhaps, a little too liberal in its approach to the complexities of the hunger problem. It is tantalizing to consider that a Communist regime, with its disregard for human rights and whims, might by being cruel, finish up by being kind. The Communists might, by one stroke, be able to destroy the prejudices and superstitions which so strangle Indian development. They might decree that the cow, monkey and rat were no longer to be treated with deified reverence, and enforce the decree. This, in itself, would produce an improvement in standards of living. The Communists would banish moneylenders, compel better methods and equable distribution. Yes, it is a tempting idea, but the final results would be too costly in other ways to contemplate.

From a purely selfish point of view—probably the most realistic trait of man to which to appeal for help—the developed countries would be doing themselves a good turn by aiding the underdeveloped ones. Paul Hoffman pointedly showed that if the backward countries were, together, given additional foreign capital and were able to increase their own savings so as to increase their *per capita* incomes by a mere 1 per cent per year for 10 years, they would provide a 14-billion-dollar market for United States exports alone.

Regrettably the work at the moment is being limited to the British organization Voluntary Service Overseas, to the United States Peace Corps and similar groups, to charitable bodies of various kinds, to some of the churches and to a few underpowered, underfinanced, underprivileged United Nations organizations. Governmental help I discount not because of its lack of volume but because it is often suspect or clumsily put into effect.

Concerted international planning is the only answer to the most urgent problem of our time.

There are great dangers in all this planning, international co-operation and systematized approach to food and population. The main one is that of the human race being ruled by social engineers in an internationally planned economy, with all its frightening visions as foreseen by George Orwell and Aldous Huxley. Is this fate preferable to mass starvation? Should you, personally, happen to be hungry your answer will be definite enough.

Let us be under no illusions about the situation. It is vast and complex and it is with us now, in acute and in chronic form. It is no longer a matter of the life of individuals being in jeopardy, but the safety of the human race.

Meanwhile, every hour of every day the human tragedies multiply. They are happening in Brazil, and Venezuela, India and Pakistan, Mauritius and Malaya—for hunger knows no frontiers.

When I was last in the Lebanon, a prosperous country in many ways, I saw in Beirut the slum area in which Arab refugees from Israel live. The Lebanese government is in no hurry to clear the slum, but prefers to maintain it as a piece of living anti-Jewish propaganda. Arab guides take all foreigners there and expound upon Jewish inhumanity, but fail to mention that Arab inhumanity to Jews is equally obnoxious. The politics of the matter are immaterial; the salient fact is that the Arabs in the Beirut slum are very poor indeed.

I was in the hills one day and found behind a rock not far from the road a newly born baby, wrapped in a shawl of sacking. Clearly the baby had not been born at the spot, but had been carried there. I assumed that it had been kidnapped and abandoned, probably out of spite. Such things do happen. I took the baby back to Beirut and asked an Arab friend to help me find the mother. Reluctantly, he agreed and after a two-day search and a lot of trouble we located the mother—a woman of about 26 living in the Beirut slum.

My self-satisfaction as I carried the infant into the tin hut was deflated by the dull look the woman gave me as she took the child. She just sat there, lifeless, cold, but said something as we left.

Outside in the sunshine I asked my friend what the woman

said. He gave me a queer look. 'She said, "Why didn't you let him die in peace? He will now only die in hunger pains." '

It is not likely that I could ever forget this incident, but I remembered it particularly when I travelled with a young Indian government doctor to a village north of Calcutta. He was on his way to treat a woman reported as seriously injured; this was one of the few reports of illness that did get through and the woman was one of the relatively few patients the doctor had time to see. She was seriously injured all right, opened up across the abdomen by something sharp and jagged. Further examination disclosed internal injuries as well. The woman, a widow aged about 30 and mother of 10 children, eight of them living, died in her hut. She was pregnant and her wounds were the result of a frantic attempt to bring about an abortion. 'It must have been just too much,' the doctor said. 'Her husband died of disease a few months ago. Two of her kids have already died from hunger, the other eight are starving and she couldn't face the prospect of another mouth to feed.'

'What will happen to the family now?' I asked.

The doctor shrugged. 'I expect they'll starve.' And half a minute later he said, 'I hope we can get back to town in time for dinner.'

You have, perhaps, taken three hours to read this book. In that time nearly 80,000 new human beings have arrived on earth. In the same time 1,360 people have died of starvation. Two in every three have been born to a life of poverty and misery.

FURTHER READING

For further reading the author recommends books he himself has found useful. They include:

The Under Privileged Nations by Pierre Mousa, Sidgwick & Jackson Ltd.

The Prevalence of People by Manston Bates, Scribners.

Conquest of the Sea by Cord-Christian Troebst, Hodder & Stoughton Ltd.

To Plough with Hope by Donald K. Faris, Victor Gollancz Ltd.

Common Sense About a Starving World by Ritchie Calder, Victor Gollancz.

2,000 Million Poor by Stephen Hearst, George G. Harrap & Son Ltd.

The Road to Survival by William Vogt, Victor Gollancz Ltd.

The Population Explosion and World Hunger by Arthur McCormack, Burns & Oates (for a Catholic viewpoint).

The Population Bomb by Dr. Paul H. Ehrlich, Ballantine Books Inc.

The Silent Explosion by Philip Appleman, Beacon Press, Boston.

Silent Spring by Rachel Carson, Houghton Mifflin Co.

Population, Evolution and Birth Control, edited by Garrett Hardin, W. H. Freeman & Co.

Our Synthetic Environment by Lewis Herber, Alfred A. Knopf Inc.

Hungry Nations by William and Paul Paddock, Little, Brown & Co.

Standing Room Only, The World's Exploding Population by Karl Sax, Beacon Press.

Famine—1975! by William and Paul Paddock, Little, Brown & Co.

Science and Survival by Barry Commoner, Viking Press.

Green Glory by Richard St. Barbe Baker, Lutterworth Press.

Also *War on Want*, a report of a conference on the U.N. Development Decade, 1962, published by Pergamon Press; *Man and Hunger* and *Statistics of Hunger*, bulletins published by the Food and Agricultural Organization, *Discovery* Magazine, London, for up-to-date information about the technological aspects of world food problems.

The author thanks, for various assistance, the U.N. Secretariat, Food and Agriculture Organization, World Health Organization, Oxfam, U.K. Freedom from Hunger Campaign and in particular its information officer, Mr. Uvedale Tristram, who wrote virtually the entire chapter on the Green Revolution for his organization's magazine, *World Hunger*. This publication is available on request from the Freedom From Hunger offices at 17 Northumberland Ave., London WC2N 5BD.

INDEX

Those subjects already listed under chapter headings are not specifically indexed

Aberdare Scheme, 227–8
Addison, Herbert, 189
Adiseshiah, Malcolm S., 18
Afghanistan, 201, 212
Africa, 24, 31, 32, 37, 40, 49, 61, 65, 69, 74, 75, 81, 82, 85, 92, 97, 100, 103, 106, 108, 111, 115, 142, 151, 155, 163, 164, 176, 179, 181, 197, 200, 201, 203
Agrawal, A. N., 119
Agricultural Education & Training (Copenhagen 1970), 110
Algeria, 84, 177
Animal diseases, 66, 73
Antarctic, 167, 179
Antilles Islands, 60
Arabian Sea, 160
Argentina, 69, 71, 149, 226
Asia, 13, 37, 40, 58, 59, 61, 65, 69, 80, 92, 97, 100, 105, 108, 130–52, 155, 179, 200; South East Asia, 24, 32, 49, 69, 71, 72, 132, 140
Association for the Advancement of Science, 171, 174
Aswan High Dam, 79
Australia, 27, 32, 48, 49, 58, 59, 64, 65, 68, 69, 71, 72, 74, 75, 82, 128, 149, 150, 151, 155, 161, 174, 177, 178, 179, 181, 184, 185, 186, 206, 226

Baker, Richard St. Barbe, 192
Belgium, 181
Bellamy, Dr. David, 159
Bevin, Ernest, 43
Bhabba, Professor Homi J., 57
Birth Control, 14, 15, 16, 17, 18, 19, 20, 46, 47, 49, 54, 55, 60, 102, 127, 129, 131, 133
Bishop, Peter, 16
Boerma, Dr. Addeke, 19, 67, 100
Bombay, 25, 76
Bond, Commander G. F., 173
Borneo, 199
Boulware, James, 128
Boyd-Orr, Lord, 14, 15, 18
Brazil, 22, 53, 65, 72, 74, 85, 103, 187, 232
Britain (see United Kingdom)
Burma, 109, 134, 136, 143, 145, 154, 202
Buss, Dr. Claude, 13

Cairo, 23, 48
Calcutta, 24, 25, 233
Calder, Professor Ritchie, 15, 19, 43, 153, 199
Cambodia, 143, 163
Cameroons, 96, 112
Canada, 48, 49, 64, 65, 69, 71, 149, 150, 226
Cant, Gilbert, 16

237

INDEX

Catholic attitude, 49
Central America, 24, 37, 92, 142
Ceylon, 46, 71, 75, 133, 142, 210, 212, 213, 223
Chambers, Robert, 17
Champagnat, A., 219
Chandra Sekhar, Dr. S., 15, 126, 127
Chile, 41, 85, 86, 90, 116, 181
China, 24, 26, 31, 34, 48, 57, 69, 72, 87, 96, 106, 117, 147, 148, 149, 150, 151, 166, 177, 192, 203, 226, 230
Chuangkashetra, Phra, 105
Cocoa, 69, 74
Coffee, 65, 69, 74
Cole, Professor G., 171
Cole, J. P., 17
Colombia, 37, 47, 65, 86
Commoner, Barry, 116
Congo, 33
Co-operative schemes, 227
Costa Rica, 53, 230
Cousteau, Jacques-Yves, 157, 166, 170
Crawford, Dr. M., 221
Cuba, 85
Cyprus, 201

Democratic govt., 139, 140
Denmark, 69, 82, 227
Disease, 19, 22, 24, 28, 33–8, 46, 73, 74, 92, 101, 121, 123, 132, 143, 165, 167, 170, 177, 190
Dobby, E. H. G., 146, 151
Dominican Republic, 163
Drought, 77, 176, 177
Dumont, René, 86

East Germany, 87, 93
Eastern Europe, 81
Ecuador, 86, 227
Egypt (see United Arab Republic)
Ehrlich, Dr. Paul H., 20, 60, 88, 178, 214
Ehrman, Dr., 189
Eire (see Ireland)
El Salvador, 53
Emigration, 51, 52, 58, 59, 60, 89
E.N.I.R., 112
Europe, 31, 32, 49, 52, 61, 65, 71, 77, 81, 82, 143, 148, 199, 200, 202, 203, 207
European Economic Community (Common Market), 49, 81, 91

Famine, 26
Far East, 31, 40, 49, 65, 75, 81, 202
Faris, Donald K., 14
Fertilizers, 31, 66, 68, 70, 96, 97, 98, 105, 148, 166, 167
Fessler, Loren, 147, 148
Finland, 185, 197
Fishing, 65, 103, 153–73
Floods, 77
Food and Agriculture Organization (F.A.O.), 15, 27, 33, 34, 41, 65, 66, 67, 68, 71, 74, 96, 97, 98, 101, 107, 108, 110, 115, 124, 136, 162, 163, 166, 168, 190, 193, 196, 198, 199,
201, 202, 203, 207, 209, 210, 212, 225, 229
Formosa (Taiwan), 34, 45, 93, 147
France, 77, 82, 89, 92, 177, 179, 185, 219
Fremlin, J. H., 53
Freudenberg, Professor Hans, 18

Gabon, 96
Gabor, Professor Denis, 16
Gal Oya Valley, 213
Gambia, 96
Gandhi, Mahatma, 14
Ghana, 37, 196
Gibraltar, 182
Greece, 28, 31, 180, 181
Guatemala, 163
Guiana, 60
Guinea, 87

Halpern, Manfred, 19
Hambridge, Dr., 71
Hardin, Garrett, 19
Hargraves, Dr. M. M., 215
Hearst, Stephen, 19
Hinduism, 49, 106
Hoffman, Paul, 19, 29, 85, 231
Holland, 51, 57, 68, 82, 190
Honduras, 163
Hong Kong, 92, 134, 149
Hoover, Herbert, 14
Hopcroft, Arthur, 47
Hot Springs Food and Agriculture Conference 1943, 15
Howard, Sir Albert, 206
Humphrey, Dr. George, 161
Hutchinson, Professor Sir Joseph, 110–11
Huxley, Sir Julian, 102
Hydroponics, 216

Icelandic Waters, 155
India, 24, 25, 26, 30, 31, 32, 33, 34, 37, 38, 43, 48, 55, 56, 57, 69, 71, 75, 76, 82, 90, 92, 96, 98, 103, 104, 106, 107, 111, 115, 117–29, 143, 157, 163, 190, 200, 202, 203, 206, 207, 210, 225
Indian National Council for Applied Economic Research, 207
Indicative World Plan, 66
Indonesia, 34, 134, 135, 137, 145, 180, 203
Intermediate Technology Organization, 99
International Development Association, 119
International Labour Organization, 62, 110
International Planned Parenthood Association, 56
Iran, 201
Iraq, 34, 69, 163, 184, 195, 196, 201
Ireland (including Eire), 50, 51, 54, 105, 185
Irrigation, 69, 96, 97, 113, 118, 147, 176, 182–90

238

INDEX

Israel, 83, 181, 186, 196, 201
Italy, 31, 51, 105, 177, 181, 185
Ivory Coast, 37

Jamaica, 33, 45
Japan, 34, 51, 55, 56, 68, 69, 70, 71,
    75, 89, 135, 145, 148, 155, 158, 159,
    167, 168, 169, 173, 203, 205, 207,
    210
Java, 72, 134, 154, 163
Jewish attitude, 106
John XXIII, Pope, 15
Jordan, 88, 163, 201
Jordan Valley, 188
Jouvenal, M. de, 212
Justicia, Dr., 227

Kalman, Dr. Sumner, 47
Kelp, 158
Kenya, 75, 77, 90, 225
Knox, Rawle, 17
Korea (South), 93, 146
Krogh, Professor August, 154
Kuwait, 180

Labour force, 61–3
Lacey, Janet, 16
Lamour, Philippe, 78
Langenskold, Mr., 214
Laos, 88, 143
Latin America, 24, 30, 32, 33, 37, 49,
    61, 69, 81, 85, 86, 92, 97, 104, 107,
    108, 142, 151, 155, 166, 177
Lawes, D. A., 208
Lebanon, 201, 232
Lewthwaite, Gilbert, 127, 128
Libya, 88, 177, 180, 211, 212
Lilienthal, David, 93
Locusts, 199–201
Lucas, Dr. C. E., 157
Lydick, J. J., 194

McKernan, D. L., 161
McMillan, Professor J. R. A., 174,
    201
McNeil, Dr. Mary, 73
Madagascar, 60, 154
Malawi, 96
Malaysia, 24, 69, 82, 137, 138, 199,
    200, 203, 223
Malta, 180
Malthus, Thomas, 52, 53, 54, 230
Mansholt, Sicco L., 142
Mauritania, 177
Mauritius, 45, 46, 134
Mead, Margaret, 16
Meade, Professor J. E., 79
Mexico, 76, 83, 98, 163, 167, 177, 185
Microbiology, 219
Monaco, 48
Moomaw, I. W., 14
Mormons, 113
Morocco, 103, 168, 182, 212
Morse, David, 61
Moussa, Pierre, 14

Nace, Dr. R. L., 175

Near East, 32, 33, 40, 41, 81, 97, 100
Nehru, Pandit, 42
New Guinea, 75, 186, 197
New York, 176
New Zealand, 27, 32, 49, 65, 69, 71,
    82, 185, 213, 226, 227
Newfoundland, 155, 197
Nicaragua, 76
Niger, 96
Nigeria, 37, 208
North America, 32, 40, 61, 65, 80, 81,
    175, 193, 199, 207
North Sea, 155
Norway, 172, 185
Notestein, 42
Nyasaland, 164

Oceania, 32, 61, 199
Oceanography: American National
    Academy of Sciences Committee on
    Oceanography, 162
Oil production, 115
Olive Fly, 201
Oswald, Dr. W. J., 169

Pakistan, 24, 26, 32, 48, 57, 69, 71, 82,
    96, 98, 107, 109, 123, 160, 163, 182,
    183, 184, 199, 200, 201, 203, 225
Palmer, Dr. C. M., 169
Panama, 167
Papua, 186
Parker, Dr. F. W., 123
Peru, 40, 85, 86, 103, 116
Petrovitch, Professor G. V., 173
Philippines, 34, 53, 75, 95, 105, 130,
    133, 138, 145, 166, 167, 199
Pirie, N. W., 15, 52, 210
Pius XII, Pope, 18
Population, 14, 15, 17, 18, 19, 20, 21,
    31, 44–53, 61, 66, 79, 83, 89, 103,
    117, 130, 131, 132, 133, 134, 135,
    149, 173, 178
Population Association, 50
Portugal, 31, 177, 202
Poultry, 202–3
Protestant attitude, 49
Puerto Rico, 45, 55

Razak Bin Hussein, Tun Abdul, 17
Récife, 22
Republic of South Africa, 40, 69, 71,
    185, 201
Réunion, 60
Rice, 25, 30, 69, 74, 95, 96, 97, 99,
    105, 113, 120, 136, 143, 148, 149,
    163, 169, 177, 205
Rinderpest, 202
Rump, Hans, 156
Russia (see U.S.S.R.)

Salonika, 28
Saudi Arabia, 180
Sen, Dr. B. R., 17, 131, 135
Seneca, 15
Senegal, 34, 96, 103, 106
Senkyevitch, Lev, 156
Sicily, 104, 108

239

INDEX

Singapore, 203
Slater, Sir William, K.B.E., 17, 20, 81
Sonar fishing, 156
South Africa, 33, 176
South America (see Latin America)
Soviet Union (see U.S.S.R.)
Soya Bean, 34, 219, 221, 224
Spain, 31, 177, 187, 202
Spilhaus, Athelstan, 20, 116, 178
Sudan, 24
Sugar, 46, 47, 74, 208, 224
Sumatra, 134
Sweden, 69, 145, 185, 197
Switzerland, 51, 69
Synthetic foods, 217 et seq., 224
Syria, 201

Tagore, Rabindranath, 144
Taiwan (see Formosa)
Tanzania, 90
Thailand, 34, 104, 112, 133, 138, 143, 145, 154, 162, 163, 203, 223
Tibet, 59
Toynbee, Professor A. J., 131
Tropical Products Institute, 226
Tropical Storage, 97
Tunisia, 37, 177, 212
Turkey, 34, 98, 201, 203
Tweddle, Donald, 16

Uganda, 90, 208
Ulrichs, Karl, 156
United Arab Republic, 23, 24, 34, 40, 69, 79, 166, 180, 184, 186, 203, 212
United Kingdom, 26, 32, 38, 39, 40, 51, 52, 53, 68, 69, 89, 91, 92, 97, 104, 109, 150, 159, 160, 166, 172, 175, 178, 181, 197, 202, 206, 207, 219
U.K. Freedom from Hunger Projects Group, 81
U.N.E.S.C.O., 103, 110, 112
U.N.I.C.E.F., 34, 107, 108, 112
United Nations, 41, 56, 66, 85, 88, 92, 110, 115, 137, 231

United Nations Development Programme, 112
United Nations Population Commission, 47
United Nations Special Fund, 29, 164, 200
United States of America, 31, 32, 38, 39, 40, 49, 50, 51, 53, 68, 69, 71, 80, 81, 82, 84, 87, 88, 89, 90, 91, 92, 96, 109, 113, 114, 116, 118, 128, 129, 143, 144, 145, 150, 160, 161, 169, 170, 171, 176, 178, 179, 180, 181, 184, 185, 194, 198, 201, 202, 206, 216, 221, 223, 226, 230, 231
United States Peace Corps, 231
Uruguay, 74, 177
U.S.S.R., 53, 61, 65, 69, 81, 84, 93, 118, 153, 155, 156, 159, 166, 167, 169, 175, 184, 186, 188, 201, 218, 219, 225, 230

Venezuela, 30, 41, 85, 197, 232
Vietnam (South), 93, 143
Virgin Islands, 180
Voluntary Service Overseas, 231

Ward, Barbara, 118
Watson, J. H. Scott, 191
West Germany, 51, 68, 69, 85, 87, 90, 118, 150
White, Teddy, 26
Winitz, Dr. M., 218
World Bank, 88, 118
World Employment Program, 62, 98
World Food Congress (Washington 1963), 76, 131; 2nd World Food Congress (The Hague, 1970), 98, 101
World Health Organization, 34, 177, 190
World Seed Campaign, 209

Young, Brigham, 113
Yugoslavia, 93, 209

Zambia, 164, 165